Past Praise for the Author's Work

"David Swanson is a truth-teller and witness-bearer whose voice and action warrant our attention." —Cornel West, author.

"David Swanson predicates his belief that nonviolence can change the world on careful research and historical analysis." — Kathy Kelly, activist and author.

"The world needs more true advocates of democracy like David Swanson!" —Thom Hartmann, radio/TV host and author.

"Our times cry out for a smart, witty and courageous Populist who hasn't forgotten how to play offense. Luckily we have David Swanson." —Mike Ferner, activist and author.

"David Swanson, who has been a one-man wonder leading the charge for accountability, writes a compelling narrative that inspires not just outrage, but ACTION." —Medea Benjamin, activist and author.

"David Swanson despises war and lying, and unmasks them both with rare intelligence. I learn something new on every page." —Jeff Cohen, activist and author.

"Swanson's book is far more uplifting and inspiring than virtually any other book in its genre, as it devotes itself to laying out a detailed plan for how American citizens—through the activism to which he has devoted himself—can l   about   rejuvenation of our political values." —Glenn Green\

"David Swanson is the most consistently great writer of this generation." —Jean Athey, activist.

"David Swanson is an antidote to the toxins of complacency and evasion. He insists on rousing the sleepwalkers, confronting the deadly prevaricators and shining a bright light on possibilities for a truly better world." —Norman Solomon, activist and author.

"I am always impressed and inspired by David's prolific energy and I admire his unwavering opposition to *all war*, not just the ones started or continued by Republicans." —Cindy Sheehan, activist and author.

"David Swanson writes like he talks; that is to say, in clear, sharp language that gets to the root of the issue, but in a very personal way...as if you are having a one-on-one conversation with him." —Leah Bolger, activist.

The author, being arrested at the White House.

War Is Never Just

by David Swanson

Charlottesville, VA
First edition—2016

Also by David Swanson
WAR IS A LIE (2010, 2016)
KILLING IS NOT A WAY OF LIFE (2014)
WAR NO MORE: THE CASE FOR ABOLITION (2013)
IRAQ WAR AMONG WORLD'S WORST EVENTS (2013)
TUBE WORLD (2012)
THE MILITARY INDUSTRIAL COMPLEX AT 50 (2011)
WHEN THE WORLD OUTLAWED WAR (2011)
DAYBREAK: UNDOING THE IMPERIAL PRESIDENCY
AND FORMING A MORE PERFECT UNION (2009)
THE 35 ARTICLES OF IMPEACHMENT (Introduction, 2008)
davidswanson.org

• • •

Swanson, David, 1969 Dec. 1-

War Is Never Just

Book design by David Swanson.
Cover photo by Ibrahem Qasim is of a destroyed house in the south of Sanaa, Yemen, on December 6, 2015, Location: 15° 17' 17" N, 44° 14' 59" E. From: https://commons.wikimedia.org

Printed in the USA
First Edition / December 2014
ISBN: 978-0-9980859-0-6

CONTENTS

INTRODUCTION

This is an attempt to persuade those not currently in agreement that there cannot ever possibly be a morally justified use of the single biggest, most expensive institution in the world, namely: war. This means that there have never been and can never be any just wars, humanitarian wars, or good wars. I expect that many will begin by not entirely agreeing. But I also expect that many have not previously considered the arguments I make below. Please consider the case I make and then contact me at davidswanson.org if you can find a hole in it.

St. Michael's College in Vermont invited me to debate/discuss the question of "Is War Necessary?" I was to take the No position. Arguing that war *is* necessary (not just any wars but particular wars that meet the right criteria) would be Mark Allman, an author of books on Just War theory. I have written my thoughts down here ahead of the debate/discussion, and am sharing them with Mr. Allman—and with you. Of course, my beliefs could end up being changed by Mark Allman, by someone else, by the course of world events, or simply by further thought, but I'm not expecting major changes in what follows.

I've been bumping up against and being unpersuaded by Just War theory for decades. My objections to it are numerous and set out below, but can be summarized in this: I believe we can end all war, I want to end all war, and Just War theory facilitates the creation and prolongation of wars.

"But doesn't a country have the right to fight back in actual defense if actually attacked?"

I will, indeed, address that question below and won't try your patience too greatly before doing so, but I need to lead up to it in a manner that brings in the entire institution of war. Just as a business that pollutes the earth can look less costly on paper than it really is, and just as a defense of torture in some extremely idiosyncratic (not to say impossible) circumstance becomes more costly if a bureaucracy is created to prepare for engaging in Just Torture (because it will engage in lots of unjust torture along the way), the promotion of the idea that there might be a Just War someday should be contemplated in conjunction with all of its costs—as well as being analyzed in terms of its theoretical merits.

The belief that we can end all wars is very far from universal, especially in the United States. I work on a project that you can find at WorldBeyondWar.org which works to persuade people of the possibility of ending all war. On that website you'll find our case that war is not inevitable, necessary, or beneficial; our proposals for alternative systems of international relations; and steps to get us there. I believe that a critical examination of Just War theory actually adds to our argument. That is, if you examine the criteria for a Just War as laid out by Just War theorists, you will be more rather than less able to accept the possibility and the need for the abolition of war.

WHAT IS A "JUST WAR"?

Just War theory holds that a war is morally justified under certain circumstances. Just War theorists lay out and elaborate upon their criteria for the just beginning of a war, the just conduct of a war, and—in some cases, including Allman's—the just occupation of conquered territories after some official announcement that a war is "over." Some Just War theorists also write about just pre-war conduct, which is helpful if it promotes behaviors that make war less likely. But no just pre-war conduct, in the view I lay out below, can justify the decision to launch a war.

Examples of Just War criteria (to be discussed below) are: right intention, proportionality, a just cause, the last resort, a reasonable prospect of success, noncombatants' immunity from attack, enemy soldiers respected as human beings, prisoners of war treated as noncombatants, war publicly declared, and war waged by a legitimate and competent authority. There are others, and not all Just War theorists agree on all of them.

Just War theory or the "Just War tradition" has been around since the Catholic Church joined up with the Roman Empire in the time of Saints Ambrose and Augustine in the fourth century CE. Ambrose opposed intermarriage with pagans, heretics, or Jews, and defended the burning of synagogues. Augustine defended both war and slavery based on his ideas of "original sin," and the idea that "this" life is of little importance in comparison with the afterlife. He believed that killing people actually helped them get to a better place and that you should never be so foolish as to engage in self-defense against someone trying to kill you.

Just War theory was further developed by Saint Thomas Aquinas in the thirteenth century. Aquinas was a supporter of slavery and of monarchy as the ideal form of government. Aquinas believed the central motive of war makers should be peace, an idea very much alive to this day, and not just in the works of George Orwell. Aquinas also thought that heretics deserved to be killed, though he believed the church should be merciful, and so preferred that the state do the killing.

Of course there was also much highly admirable about these ancient and medieval figures. But their Just War ideas fit better with their worldviews than with ours. Out of an entire perspective (including their views of women, sex, animals, the environment, education, human rights, etc., etc.) that makes little sense to most of us today, this one piece called "Just War theory" has been kept alive well beyond its expiration date.

Many advocates of Just War theory no doubt believe that by promoting criteria for a "just war" they are taking the inevitable horror of war and mitigating the damage, that they are making unjust wars a little bit less unjust or maybe even a lot less unjust, while making sure that just wars are begun and are properly executed. "Necessary" is a word that Just War theorists should not object to. They cannot be accused of calling war good or pleasant or cheerful or desirable. Rather, they claim that some wars can be necessary—not physically necessary but morally justified although regrettable. If I shared that belief, I would find courageous risk-taking in such wars to be noble and heroic, yet still unpleasant and undesirable—and thus in only a very particular sense of the word: "good."

The majority of the supporters in the United States of particular wars are not strict Just War theorists. They may believe a war is in some manner defensive, but have typically not thought through whether it's a "necessary" step, a "last resort." Often they are very open about seeking revenge, and often about targeting for revenge ordinary non-combatants, all of which is rejected by Just War theory. In some wars, but not others, some fraction of supporters also believe the war is intended to rescue the innocent or bestow democracy and human rights on the afflicted. In 2003 there were Americans who wanted Iraq bombed in order to kill a lot of Iraqis, and Americans who wanted Iraq bombed in order to liberate Iraqis from a tyrannical government. In 2013 the U.S. public rejected its government's pitch to bomb Syria for the supposed benefit of Syrians. In 2014 the U.S. public supported bombing Iraq and Syria to supposedly protect themselves from ISIS. According to much of recent Just War theory it shouldn't matter who is being protected. To most of the U.S. public, it matters very much.

While there are not enough Just War theorists to launch a war without lots of help from unjust war advocates, elements of Just War theory are found in the thinking of just about every war supporter. Those thrilled by a new war will still call it "necessary." Those eager to abuse all standards and conventions in the conduct of the war will still condemn the same by the other side. Those cheering for attacks on non-threatening nations thousands of miles away will never call it aggression, always "defense" or "prevention" or "preemption" or punishment of misdeeds. Those explicitly denouncing or evading the United Nations will still claim that their government's wars uphold rather than drag down the rule of law. While Just War theorists are far from agreeing with each other on all points, there are some common themes, and they work to facilitate the waging of war in general—even though most or all of the wars are unjust by the standards of Just War theory.

JUST WAR THEORY FACILITATES UNJUST WARS

Once a war has begun, I can certainly agree with every argument for restraint except in so far as it works against ending the war. Just War thinking can be used to argue against restraint: it's better to make sure the war succeeds quickly than to prolong it. But Just War thinking is often used in favor of restraint, and has, I believe, been central to the creation of the Geneva Conventions and all variety of standards, treaties, laws, rules, and common practices.

It's not entirely clear whether Just War arguments have ever been used in a crisis to prevent or significantly restrain a particular war. In the spring of 2016, when the Catholic Church was holding a meeting in Rome on rejecting the idea of a Just War,[1] a blogger named *Ken Sehested asked me if I could name a time when Just War theory had been used to prevent or drastically rein in a war. Then he published this:*

> "*In preparation for this article I wrote fifty people—pacifists and just warriors alike, academics-to-activists, who know something about the use of just war theory—asking if they could cite evidence of a potential war averted (or significantly altered) due to the constraints of just war*

criteria. More than half responded, and not a single one could name a case. What's more surprising is the number who considered my question a novel one. If the just war matrix is to be an honest broker of policy decisions, surely there must be verifiable metrics."[2]

I had stressed to Sehested, as I will discuss below, that some of the criteria of Just War theory are not empirical. They cannot be measured. One cannot know whether they have been met or not. This makes it difficult to use Just War theory in opposition or support of particular wars.

But Just War theory is part of Western culture. It would be hard to prove that any restraint in war making wasn't influenced by it. I think Just War theory has been very much a part of establishing certain standards that are sometimes partially complied with. In Mark Allman and Tobias Winright's book *After the Smoke Clears: The Just War Tradition & Post War Justice* (2010), which extends the arguments found in Allman's *Who Would Jesus Kill? War, Peace, and the Christian Tradition* (2008), the authors refer to "the ugly reality that all sides commit crimes *in bello*."[3] The Latin term *in bello*, of course, refers to conduct during a war, as opposed to *ad bellum*, which refers to arguments for initiating a war. The authors are admitting here that all wars are unjust, to one degree or another, in their conduct. Allman and Winright may still suppose that, theoretically, that need not be so. Whether they believe any war in history has ever been just *ad bellum*, I couldn't make out from their book, but they certainly maintain that in theory a war could be (despite the certainty or near certainty that said war will be conducted unjustly). In a 2016 article, they do suggest that justly begun wars have existed, and seem to hint that they used to be more common:

> "*Even if the case for just war is rare, such cases still occur: specific examples include Rwanda and Kosovo, as recognized by the United Nations in its recent R2P norm for international relations. Another would be the threat posed by ISIS to Christians and others in Iraq and Syria, extreme situations from which perpetrators and victims alike need to be rescued.*"[4]

I'll address the unjustness of these three examples and others toward the end of this book. I'll just note here that two of the three are wars that have not happened. The first is Rwanda, where militarism created a slaughter that humanitarian warriors regret not having addressed with more militarism. The second is a war that eliminates a threat posed by ISIS—a war that doesn't sound much like a war at all, as rescuing both perpetrators and victims seems at odds with, you know, *waging war* against the perpetrators. I will address the unjustness of existing war making against ISIS below. The third case is Kosovo, a war whose justness I will challenge below. Let me just note here that for every Kosovo that someone claims was a Just War or a justly begun war (even if unjustly conducted), there are dozens and dozens of wars about which few if any Just War theorists make that claim.

And that's a problem. I suspect that I could list hundreds of wars that many Just War theorists would agree with me should never have been launched. Heck, I can do that with the majority of the

U.S. public, at least with the wars people have heard of. In 2001 and 2003 a majority or close to it in U.S. polls favored two particular big new wars. But within about a year and a half after each of those wars was begun (in Afghanistan and Iraq), and ever since, polls have found a majority in the U.S. saying those wars, which still haven't ended, should not have been started. Yet, the idea that there might be a just war at some point in the future has majority support and enormous consequences, some of them, as I'm about to explain, more deadly than any individual war we've ever seen.

Allman and Winright claim it is unfair to ask whether there has ever been a just war, suggesting that a moral ideal is valuable whether or not it has ever been met.[5] Yet it is the idea that there could be a just war that props up massive military spending and support for endless unjust wars. We cannot easily dismantle or even restrain the Pentagon—the largest and most destructive institution in the United States and the world—without deciding whether or not it might ever serve a worthy purpose, and whether the need to be prepared for that possibility outweighs all the demonstrable harm brought about by the preparations.

Often the idea that there might be a just war in the future is boosted by the notion that there has been one or some small number of just wars in the past, or that there could have been one but the opportunity was missed. World War II plays such a dominant role in this that I am including some specifics on why World War II was not a just war toward the end of this book. I've written and spoken at length elsewhere about World War II, the U.S. Revolution, the U.S. Civil War, the war on Yugoslavia over

Kosovo, and various other candidates for a Just War, including two that didn't happen: Rwanda and Sudan.[6] I will include a summary of the unjustness of each of these near the end of this book.

I think it is telling that the vast majority of such arguments reach back 75 years to World War II and a dramatically different world, and that wars that did not happen play such a major supporting role. In 2011 we were told that Libya needed to be bombed because of Rwanda. But in 2013 we were not told that Syria needed to be bombed because of Libya. U.S. Ambassador to the United Nations Samantha Power urged us to ignore the disaster that bombing had created in Libya so that we might properly support bombing Syria . . . again, because of Rwanda.[7]

Of course, everything should have been done differently in Rwanda, including refraining from the militarism of the years that led up to what is meant by "Rwanda,"—and the militarism that continued into the far larger horrors in the Congo that nobody talks about or seems to hold any deep regret over. But never would bombing have helped, and had it been tried, Rwanda would not be the example anybody would appeal to. As military-driven nation-building and humanitarian wars have not yet built a nation or benefited humanity, their advocates will continue to lean heavily on the wars that did not happen.

I won't take up the space here to discuss each possible candidate for a past Just War. See below. But, while I've found every war I've examined to be grossly unjust, by the standards of Just War theory and by my own standards, even were we to all agree that one out of every fifty wars has been just, that would not outweigh the damage done by war preparations and the 49 unjust wars that accompany war preparations. Much less would the potential of a first-ever Just War at some point down the road (should we survive long enough) outweigh the destruction done by keeping the institution of war around.

PREPARING FOR A JUST WAR IS A GREATER INJUSTICE THAN ANY WAR

It's little noted but, I think, very clear that for all the damage done by all the recent wars, more damage has been done by the preparation for them. War rivals climate change and all diseases as a top cause of death and suffering in the world. And preparing for war clearly makes war more, rather than less, likely. But the preparation itself is more deadly than the wars. This is because the world invests roughly $2 trillion per year in preparing for and waging wage, at least 90% of it in preparing for wars, and roughly half of it from the United States alone[8], another huge portion from close U.S. allies, and the biggest chunk on U.S.-made weapons. It would cost about $30 billion per year to end starvation and hunger around the world. That sounds like a lot of money to you or me. But if we had $2 trillion it would sound like small change. And we do, as long as we're making moral choices about whether preparing for wars is just.

It would cost about $11 billion per year to provide the world with clean water. Again, that sounds like a lot. Let's round up to $50 billion per year to provide the world with both food and water.

Who has that kind of money? We do. A U.S. Air Force expert was quoted in the spring of 2016 explaining that the United Nations was failing to drop food near starving people in Syria. The Air Force, he said, had the technology to drop food accurately from high altitude in high wind but would never use it for a purely humanitarian operation because it costs $60,000.[9] Each missile that the United States throws at Western Asia like confetti costs $1,400,000, but as a matter of principle, the U.S. military won't spend $60,000 on something that doesn't kill anybody, that merely saves their lives. Why is the military in charge of dropping food on people anyway? Because it's in charge of almost everything—it's where the money goes.

Of course, we in the wealthier parts of the world don't share money, even among ourselves. Those in need of aid are right here as well as far away. But imagine if the United States were to put $500 billion into its own educational needs (meaning that "college debt" would soon begin to sound as backward as "human sacrifice"), housing (meaning no more people without homes), infrastructure, and sustainable green energy and agricultural practices (meaning a possible future for humanity on Earth). What if, instead of leading the destruction of the natural environment, this country were catching up and helping to lead in the other direction? The potential of green energy would suddenly skyrocket with that sort of unimaginable investment, and the same investment again, year after year. Even $400 billion at first, or $200 billion, or $20 billion would make a major difference.

What about a similar investment in providing the world with green energy and infrastructure, topsoil preservation, environmental protection, schools, medicine, programs of cultural exchange, agriculture, clean water, and the study of peace and of nonviolent action? U.S. foreign aid right now is about $23 billion a year, not counting free weapons. Increasing non-military foreign aid to $100 billion or several times that would have a number of interesting impacts, including the saving of a great many lives and the prevention of a tremendous amount of suffering. It would also, if one other factor were added, make the nation that did it the most beloved nation on earth. A 2013 poll of people in 65 nations found that the United States was far and away the most feared country, the country considered the largest threat to peace in the world.[10] Were the United States responsible for providing schools and medicine and solar panels, that would change, and the idea of anti-American terrorist groups would be as laughable as anti-Swiss or anti-Costa Rican terrorist groups, but only if one other factor were added—only if the funding came from where it really ought to come from, and the only place it *can* come from: the budget for war preparations.

Many Just War theorists might agree with enhanced investing in human and environmental needs, in systems of arbitration and justice, in truth and reconciliation commissions, in foreign aid and diplomacy and cooperation. They might support what they call building "just peace." In some cases they support such measures, modeled on the Marshall Plan (one hopes without its flaws), as the just way to follow through on a war. One would hope that they would also support the same positive steps in the absence of having waged a war first. The problem is that the resources needed for this project are all tied up in preparations for more wars. And even if significant, though not equivalent, resources were obtained by taxing the super-wealthy, the project of bringing aid and friendship to nations would be in conflict with the project of building U.S. military bases in nations. There are U.S. troops now in 175 countries out of roughly 200 on earth, in many cases in large numbers, and in many of those cases deeply resented, and in some of those cases routinely protested. Any investment in preparations for peace will find itself bumping up against these preparations for war.

Shifting money away from war spending would not be an economic sacrifice. If it meant fewer wars, that would mean the savings of trillions of dollars globally in wars' destruction each year.[11] Even without reducing the number of wars, it would mean more jobs, better paying jobs, and stronger economic impact if invested in peaceful industries or even tax cuts for ordinary people. University of Massachusetts economists have found that military spending is worse economically than nothing, worse than never taxing money in the first place.[12] Yet it takes up over half of U.S. federal discretionary spending each year.[13]

Based on the theory that there might be a Just War someday, the U.S. government has created a Frankenstein monster in the form of the Military Industrial Complex. I haven't seen any theories of Just War Profiteering, but the war profiteers set the agenda.[14] As Arundhati Roy has noted, "Once weapons were manufactured to fight wars. Now wars are manufactured to sell weapons." Not only do U.S. war profiteers shape U.S. government spending and foreign policy, but they employ the U.S. State Department as a very powerful marketing firm to gain weapons contracts from other governments all over the world—governments of all sorts from representative to royal.[15] As a result, the United States has become the leading arms dealer to the world.[16] Regions that Americans think of as inherently violent are primarily armed with U.S. weapons. Like alcohol to the Native Americans and opium to the Chinese, guns are now pushed on the world's poor. Groups that Americans think of as barbaric, such as ISIS, parade with U.S. vehicles and guns. Wars without U.S. weaponry on both sides are the exception. Troops armed by the U.S. Department of so-called Defense and troops armed by the U.S. Central so-called Intelligence Agency have lately been fighting and killing each other in Syria.[17] Of course, Just War academics didn't pull those triggers, but the arms industry would not survive the demise of the theory that some wars can be justified.

What is a Just Arms Industry? I'm sure I do not know, but the unjust arms industry is propped up by Just War theory, and one can imagine how the arguments would play out. If innocent people might be victimized by aggressors, we have a responsibility to either wage war on their behalf or arm them, whichever measure will be the most "proportional" and have the most "right intention" and so forth. (We'll be discussing all such criteria shortly.) Pope Francis in 2015 told a joint session of the U.S. Congress to end the arms trade, told them in fact that they had blood on their hands. And they cheered. And then they expanded the arms trade.

"Being at the service of dialogue and peace," he said, "also means being truly determined to minimize and, in the long term, to end the many armed conflicts throughout our world. Here we have to ask ourselves: Why are deadly weapons being sold to those who plan to inflict untold suffering on individuals and society? Sadly, the answer, as we all know, is simply for money: money that is drenched in blood, often innocent blood. In the face of this shameful and culpable silence, it is our duty to confront the problem and to stop the arms trade."[18]

Just War theory appeals to the same logic that suggests there could someday be a Just Arms Industry. While weapons rarely remain with their first purchaser, the second and third owners would not have been "intended."[19] While arms sales often provoke an arms race, only one side of the arms race would have to claim "just" status, although in reality both, independently of each other, always do.

Financial trade offs and the military industrial complex are just the beginning of the costs of war preparation. Public dollars spent on war preparations find their way into movies, video games, advertisements, school science fairs, and a million other avenues through which our culture is corrupted into an acceptance of mass violence. In order to buy yet more weapons, the old weapons are given to local police forces, and bureaucracies developed to train police to treat the public as an enemy, and non-violent activists as potential terrorists. The steady flow of war after war against areas of the world dominated by particular ethnic and religious groups fuels vicious racism and bigotry at home (and *vice versa*). The furious flow of fear used to build war support also facilitates the stripping away of civil liberties, first for targeted groups and then for nearly everyone. Shouts of "freedom!" surrounding wars fail to obscure the steady losses in freedom.

I've saved the worst three consequences of upholding the institution of war for last. First, the war machine is the single biggest threat to the natural environment of the earth. Second, the wars it generates endanger us rather than making us safer. Third, the existence of nuclear weapons threatens all human and much other life on earth. See the WorldBeyondWar.org website for documentation of each of these points and those above. Not only does war suck up critical resources needed to protect the earth and its climate, but preparations for and the waging of war do more damage to our environment than any other human activity.

Not only does war fail to make us safe, but it is counterproductive, endangering those whose government commits it. I'll just include here a few citations related to this point:

- Former CIA Bin Laden Unit Chief Michael Scheuer says the more the U.S. fights terrorism the more it creates terrorism.
- U.S. Lt. General Michael Flynn, who quit as head of the Pentagon's Defense Intelligence Agency in 2014, says blowing people up with missiles is generating more blowback, not less.
- The CIA's own July 7, 2009, report "Best Practices in Counterinsurgency," says drone killing is counterproductive.
- Admiral Dennis Blair, a former director of National Intelligence, says the same.
- Gen. James E. Cartwright, a former vice chairman of the Joint Chiefs of Staff, says drone strikes could be undermining long-term efforts: "We're seeing that blowback. If you're trying to kill your way to a solution, no matter how precise you are,

you're going to upset people even if they're not targeted."

- Dozens of just retired top officials echo this theme.[20]

There is little question that the war on terrorism is not ending terrorism.[21] There should be little question that the purported goal of ending terrorism is not the actual goal of many of the decision makers who have waged the U.S. wars of the past 15 years, and not even the actual goal of many of these wars' ordinary supporters. One can imagine the wars, occupations, invasions, and drone strikes that a country like Mexico or Uruguay or Canada or Kyrgyzstan would have to commit before it could become the target of hatred and violence that the United States and some of its allies have become. War produces the supposed need for war, not the other way around. When Spain experienced blowback in 2004 it pulled out of the war on Iraq; the Islamist terrorism in Spain ended. When the U.K. and France experienced blowback, they doubled down on wars; the terrorism against them increased.

Added to any calculation that involves the maintenance or abolition of the institution of war must be the threat that nuclear weapons pose to life on this planet. While they could be abolished and other weaponry and wars be retained, they could not be retained were war abolished.

JUST WAR CULTURE
JUST MEANS MORE WAR

Now, surely it's not fair of me to hold a Just War theorist in the United States responsible for the extent of the injustice engaged in by the U.S. government in the course of its unjust wars, while blaming a Just War theorist in Iceland (if there be such a person) for so much less, when the two of them may propound nearly identical theories. Well, maybe, maybe not. Maybe it's worse to yell "fire!" in a crowded theater than in a deserted park. I'm not really interested in handing out blame to anyone. I suspect, however, that you will find a greater presence of Just War theorists in the United States and other heavily militarized countries than you will elsewhere, just as you find a greater presence of people who claim to pollsters that they "would" participate in a war. According to a Gallup poll in 2014, 68 percent of Italians polled said they would *not* fight for their country, while 20 percent said they would. In Germany 62 percent said they would not, while 18 percent said they would. In the Czech Republic (aka Czechia), 64 percent would not fight for their country, while 23 percent would. In the Netherlands, 64 percent would not fight for their country, while 15 percent would. In Belgium, 56 percent would not, while 19 percent would. Even in the U.K., 51 percent would not participate in a U.K. war, while 27 percent would. In France, Iceland, Ireland, Spain, and Switzerland, more people would refuse to be part of a war than would agree. The same goes for Australia and Canada. In Japan only 10 percent would fight for their country.

Despite waging the greatest number of baseless and costly wars, the United States manages 44 percent claiming a willingness to fight and 31 percent refusing. By no means is that the world record. Israel is at 66 percent ready to fight and 13 percent not. Afghanistan is at 76 to 20. Russia, Sweden, Finland, and Greece are all ready to fight with strong majorities, with or without (I suspect with) their fair share of Just War theorists.[22]

Rose Marie Berger, who participated in the meeting at the Vatican this past April, on the topic of switching from "Just War" to "Just Peace," told me, "There was a particular 'ah-ha' moment at the Rome conference on nonviolence when the Western European academics realized that the participants from Africa and the Middle East didn't know what 'just war theory' was, even though almost all of them were on the receiving end of wars initiated or funded by Western powers. It became clear in conversation that Western seminaries teach 'just war' as the exclusive framework on war and peace issues, while it was barely touched on in African seminaries. To me it appears that just war theory has become the exclusive domain of empires, while the church in 'client countries' tends toward pragmatic nonviolence as is emphasized in the peace section of Catholic catechism and clearly demonstrated in the gospels."[23]

Perhaps Just War theory, born of empire, lives best in empire. Really, what use would a nation with no imperial ambitions have for it?

Many western academics like to think of war as arising out of other cultures, not their own. Theories speculate that war is created by population density or resource scarcity or climate change or inequality or Islam or communism. Yet the science on this seems pretty clear. While anything can be used as the immediate cause of / excuse for a war, the same conflict would not produce a war in a culture that didn't accept war. The only factor that actually correlates with the tendency to go to war is cultural acceptance of war.[24]

Just War and related theories have positive influences, no doubt. They attempt to discourage some wars and to mitigate certain nasty aspects of all wars. Many people would prefer to have wars without torture, for example. I don't disagree. Except in two senses. First, replacing torture with murder as the standard approach to targeted individuals, as President Barack Obama has done with his drone kill list—killing, in fact, many individuals who we know could have been easily arrested had that been desired[25]—has been described to me by a former CIA employee as "cleaner."[26] I assume most Just War theorists would agree with me that it is worse or as bad or nearly as bad to murder someone as to torture them. And when we consider the numbers of people involved, and that some 90% of the people killed by missiles from U.S. drones were not "targeted" people at all, the impact begins to look worse.[27]

Then there's this question: why can't there exist Just Torture? (Or for that matter, why not Just Drone Murders?) Surely if you can have Just War, you can have Just Torture or Just Assassination by very similar logic. In fact, I think that Just Torture and Just War have in common that they can't be found in reality but can be made to work very well in theory. In theory, and in Hollywood, you can know that someone knows information that will save many lives, and that torturing them is the best hope to produce that information. In reality, rarely will you know what others have in their heads, rarely will torture be the fastest and most reliable way to extract it (especially if a time bomb is ticking), never will you *know* that torture is the best approach to try, and yet over and over again people authorized to attempt Just Torture will engage in unjust torture with all the accompanying and corrupting results.

Similarly, murder by drone missile or non-drone missile is preferred over the use of chemical or biological weapons by many with Just War tendencies because in theory the former can be less indiscriminate, even though in reality, thus far, that is simply not the case.

As we will see in the discussion of Just War criteria that follows, as with torture or assassination, it is also possible to imagine a Just *War* in theory, but impossible to produce or identify one in practice.

The second objection I have to proposing war without torture (other than the difficulty of getting it, given the mental state required for participation in war) is the same objection I have to all such refinements. They suggest that mass murder can be acceptable, that there can be a proper way to do it. "Even War Has Rules!" is a graphic that shows up on my computer after every bombing of a hospital or school. But should it? Do other forms of murder have rules? We don't have Geneva Conventions for rape or theories of Just Slavery or codes of proper and humane child abuse. Some things are set aside as evil in their entirety. (Until recently, in U.S. academia, torture was often one of them.) Unless war, the institution of war, can be morally justified, then it too is evil—and normalizing it with standards and regulations, for whatever good that may do, also does the evil work of making war acceptable.

One could imagine the United States scaling its military back to the proportionate size of, say, Italy's or Australia's, abolishing nuclear and chemical and biological weapons, closing foreign bases, scrapping weaponry that lacks a defensive purpose, and yet continuing to maintain and plan for a military defense of the actual United States, even while the bulk of the military budget was redirected to human and environmental needs. And one could imagine elements of Just War theory continuing to exist in such a world. But so-called humanitarian wars, the "Responsibility to Protect," the bombing of another Yugoslavia, would have to be foregone by a Department of Defense that had decided to limit itself to defense of its own nation. Of course, the protection of actually endangered people could be pursued by other agencies through nonviolent means; it just couldn't serve as the means of launching wars. I also predict that we would see an arms reduction race take off if the United States led it, with each nation buying and selling less and less weaponry. Gradually, the need for an academic field of war regulation would come to look as relevant as Advanced Studies in Dueling or Trial by Ordeal.

In the world we live in, the existence of Just War theory allows the mongers of every war to claim that their particular violence is just. As Allman and Winright note, "The Bush administration pitched the wars in Afghanistan and Iraq to the American people and to the world as just wars."[28] The idea that mass murder might be just is what allowed U.S. Secretary of State Madeleine Albright to claim that killing 500,000 children was "worth it."[29] It's also what allowed the following. In December 2015, in a CNN presidential debate, one of the moderators asked: "We're talking about ruthless things tonight. Carpet bombing, toughness, war, and people wonder, could you do that? Could you order airstrikes that would kill innocent children, not scores but hundreds and thousands. Could you wage war as a commander in chief?"[30] I expect many

Just War theorists would recognize that killing thousands of innocent children has become the norm, not just a theory, for U.S. presidents, while the possibility of doing so somehow justly is remote in the extreme. If in practice Just War theory facilitates unjust wars, then the just war theorist must avoid articulating his or her theory aloud or putting it in writing. (I am not advocating self-censorship of something that I find persuasive and convincing: the theory is also incoherent on its own terms. I will come back to this shortly.)

In response to an "appeal" by others, Allman and Winright recently wrote: "Of course, the appeal's main criticism can't be denied: 'Too often the "just-war theory" has been used to endorse rather than prevent or limit war.' But this is not a problem with just-war thinking per se; it is problem with how it is used."[31] That last assertion contains some truth, although there are indeed problems with the theory. The trouble is that keeping the theory around makes it very likely to continue being misused. And, in fact, misused is all that it can be, as using it is really not possible. To understand this, we must examine the various Just War criteria.

THE AD BELLUM / IN BELLO DISTINCTION DOES HARM

It is common to divide Just War criteria into those arguments used for justly starting a war and those for justly conducting the war. These are called, respectively, *jus ad bellum* and *jus in bello*. David Carroll Cochran, in *Catholic Realism and the Abolition of War,* refers to such talk as the following two categories of lies:

mendacia ad bellum (war launching lies) and *mendacia in bello* (mid-war lies).[32] I'm going to look at some *ad bellum* and *in bello* justice or lying criteria, as the case may be, lumped together, as I want to group the criteria into three other categories: the non-empirical, the impossible, and the amoral.

In my 2010 book, *War Is A Lie,* I look at types of lies used to start wars, such as "They will attack us if we don't attack them," and lies to continue wars, such as "We owe it to the troops who have already died to kill more troops." In Just War theory, neither standard category, *ad bellum* nor *in bello*, really corresponds to arguments for continuing a war. This seems primarily to be because once a war has been launched a discussion of ending it is often not deemed acceptable at all. Instead the *in bello* category covers the proper details of the manner of conduct, regardless of whether it was just to begin a war, and even more regardless of whether it is just to continue it. The reasonable-prospect-of-success criterion ought to be applied at every instant during a war as war makers decide whether or not to continue the war; instead its consideration seems to be theorized only at the start of a war.

Allman and Winright, among others, also propose the category of *post bellum* for considering the proper occupation of a conquered people and the state of affairs that must be created before a foreign military can "justly" cease such an occupation. (Apparently, an occupying army should create a peaceful, democratic government, achieve reconciliation, punish itself for its invasion, restore the rule of law, and clean up after itself, all while continuing the occupation.) It appears to me that this calculation is made, in

Allman and Winright's theory, regardless of whether the people occupied appreciate it or not, and regardless of whether achieving the specified state of affairs is plausibly ever going to happen. They make no mention of allowing public votes on whether the occupation should continue. They create no requirement that examples of successful nation-building have been achieved in the past—or even have been remotely approached.

Dividing the question of a Just War into *ad bellum* and *in bello* seems to me to have a number of additional drawbacks. It allows someone to claim that launching a war is "just" even while knowing that it will almost certainly be conducted unjustly. The same distinction, coming from the other direction, allows for setting aside the question of whether a war is justly begun or continued, in order to focus on whether it is being properly conducted. Imagine if Canada invaded the United States for (as with any invasion) no good reason. Then imagine Canadian "human rights groups" publishing studies on the "just" conduct of the war in terms of treatment of prisoners, absence of torture, and the honest-really-truly-not-kidding intention only to target actual combatants resisting the occupation when launching each and every missile into U.S. cities. Such a scenario might raise a number of unusual questions in the mind of a U.S. citizen:

1. Can such an outrage possibly be properly continued?
2. Why is it OK to target those who resist such an outrage?
3. If the Canadians know civilians will die, how can they claim with a straight face not to have intended it?
4. Which humans do human rights groups give a damn about?

But, thanks to the *ad bellum / in bello* distinction, this is exactly what prominent Western human rights groups do with U.S. and NATO wars in other parts of the world. Amnesty International, Human Rights Watch, the ACLU, and others will tell you that, as a matter of principle, they take no position on the legality or morality of beginning any war; they look only at the *in bello* conduct of the war in order to try to improve it.[33] And who can oppose that, except in so far as it diverts us from the possibility that ending the war might be superior to improving it?

SOME JUST WAR CRITERIA ARE NOT MEASURABLE

The Just War criteria that are not measurable include:
1. Right Intention
2. Just Cause
3. Proportionality

RIGHT INTENTION

A national government is not a human being. It is hard enough to pin down one's own intentions, much less those of another human being. But those of a government are extremely difficult to identify, isolate, and believe. What qualifies as a "right" intention in Just War theory is something nations often do not even pretend to. A government may in some sense claim just intentions, but officials' private discussions vary dramatically from their public statements. Sometimes a war is presented publicly as more "just," as with the 2011 overthrow of the Libyan government being presented as a humanitarian rescue mission, while reading then-Secretary of State Hillary Clinton's emails suggests motivations more related to oil, economics, and geo-politics.[34] Other times, bureaucrats may discuss the pointlessness of a war, as happened in meetings about the Vietnam War exposed in the Pentagon Papers, but the end result of such meetings may be the continuation of the war, not to resist the enemy as depicted in the propaganda but simply to "save face" for the moment by not ending the war yet.[35]

President George W. Bush at times suggested that within the War on Iraq that began in 1990 and hasn't ended, the stage that began in 2003 was intended as revenge for Saddam Hussein's alleged (and likely fictitious) role in an assassination attempt against Bush's father[36], and at other times Bush revealed that God had told him what to do.[37] After bombing Vietnam, Lyndon Johnson supposedly gloated: "I didn't just screw Ho Chi Minh, I cut his pecker off." According to George Stephanopoulos, Bill Clinton had this to say about Somalia in 1993:

> *"We're not inflicting pain on these fuckers. When people kill us, they should be killed in greater numbers. I believe in killing people who try to hurt you. And I can't believe we're being pushed around by these two-bit pricks."*[38]

In May 2003, *New York Times* columnist Thomas Friedman summed up elite U.S. support for war on Iraq when he said on the *Charlie Rose Show* on PBS, that the purpose of the war was to send U.S. troops door-to-door in Iraq to say 'Suck on this.'"

For any given war, one can find key officials articulating intentions as unjust as any of these, and key officials—often the very same ones—articulating quintessentially just intentions. Even assuming that one could work out the dominant or sincere majority intentions in a legislature or executive, there is the practical problem that the more just motivations tend to be publicly propounded earlier, while the less just motivations often leak out years after the fact. In 2002 anyone suggesting that a war on Iraq would be about oil had a very hard time getting on U.S. television, while in 2016, we can read in the Chilcot Report that the war was (is?) very much about oil.[39] How can I, as a civilian and supposed sovereign of a so-called representative government ask to be properly represented in my view of the justness of a war, in a timely manner, if I can't reliably make out what the intentions are? How could anyone in any utopian government that might be created?

The criterion of right intention seems, in practice, both in the moment and after the fact, to be in part an argument from authority and from credulity. One must judge the intentions of the war makers based on what they tell you. And if the hundreds of members of Congress profess to a mish-mash of conflicting motivations ("protect Syrians" and "overthrow the Syrian government" and "take a step toward overthrowing the Iranian government" and "create weapons jobs in my district" and "make a statement against killing children by bombing children" and "punish Muslims") one must pick some coherent set of intentions on no clear basis and then decide if it's "right" or not. One can imagine a much more "just" war than most current wars, but it is much more difficult to imagine everyone agreeing on what that war is for.

While consideration of intentions seems relevant to the behavior of individuals, it does not seem to work when applied to a government or a military. When one adds all the people actually participating in the war to the calculation of right intent, it becomes infinitely more confused. Even in a war most plausibly characterized as defensive, no individual soldier is behaving defensively by participating, since the most defensive action, at least in the near-term, for that soldier would be to desert. Participating in a war means putting yourself at risk in order to kill other people who themselves probably had little or nothing to do with the actions used to justify the war, and in order to take home a paycheck, among many other more and less noble motivations. Is that a right or non-right intention?

If one soldier intends to defend his country, another intends to spread democracy, another intends to kill Muslims, and 20 more intend to defend those three and each other, whose intentions do we look at? Does it matter if the likely outcome is endangering their country, or if the chances of spreading democracy are less than those of spreading leukemia, or if none of the soldiers would have to intend to defend each other if there were no war? And what if war intentions, both in White House meetings and in actual combat, tend to rely on *irrational* intentions? Can those intentions be "right"?

Jane Addams, the great peace activist and social worker, in a speech in New York during World War I, said that in countries she'd visited in Europe, young soldiers had said that it was difficult to make a bayonet charge, to kill other young men up close, unless "stimulated"—that the English were given rum, the Germans ether, and the French absinthe. That this was a hopeful indication that men weren't all natural murderers, and the fact that it was accurate, were brushed aside in the attacks on Addams' "slander" of the sainted troops, attacks that nearly drove her into despairing retirement. In fact U.S. soldiers who participate in today's wars die more from suicide than any other cause, and efforts to suppress their moral injury may have made them the most medicated killers in history.[40] They're drugged to allow additional "tours" of "duty," but are they drugged to have the right intentions?

The government in which one could best identify a "right intention" in going to war would be one in which a single individual makes the decision—the sort of government that Aquinas favored. Justly or otherwise, that is increasingly how the U.S. government is viewed. But in reality, even in the starkest dictatorship, multiple people have influence on such a decision. And any government is very likely to take into account the interests of its particular nation. This makes a certain sense when proposing the idea of a defensive war, but not when suggesting the justness of a humanitarian or philanthropic war. In both cases the Just War theorist requires that a nation act in the interests of all humanity, and in the latter the nation is supposed to make sacrifices on behalf of people outside the nation. In reality, even when a nation can somehow be understood to act with altruistic intentions, it will certainly still be acting with selfish intentions as well. The supra-national force that could meet the standards of Just War theory does not exist and would have a hard time motivating enthusiasm for wars if it did.

JUST CAUSE

At first glance, "just cause" seems more empirical than "right intention," since, in order to be something other than "right intention," the criterion of "just cause" has to refer to the foreseeable results of a war rather than the intentions of its human planners or the "intention" of an entity like a government. (When "just cause" is taken to mean "right intention" in a broader and more long-term perspective, it faces the same problems as "right intention.") But any war has numerous likely results, with some of those results easily characterized as just. Does a war that is likely to do a hillock of good and a mountain of harm count as "just"? Where's the balance?

According to Allman and Winright, "[w]ar is seen as legitimate if it is waged in self-defense, to protect the innocent, in defense of human rights, or in response to acts of aggression."[41] Is a war launched after being attacked self-defense? What about one launched preemptively? What about one to rid another nation of weapons? What war could not claim to be protecting the innocent or defending human rights? What nation that might be attacked isn't violating some human rights? And what are we to make of "in response to acts of aggression," which has nothing to do with future results, dealing rather with the recent past? How does launching a "just" war against a nation because its government committed some past act of aggression differ from "unjust" revenge?

That distinction seems to usually be simply a matter of hypocritical double standards. If your nation attacks a bad country, doing so is law-enforcement, even if the war is illegal. If another country attacks yours, well then, that's evil rogue aggression to be punished with vengeance, er, I mean, with law enforcement. After they quote Cicero saying that revenge justifies war, Allman and Winright explain: "Although Cicero used the word 'revenge' . . . he probably had in mind bringing the guilty party to justice, so that the punishment would fit the offense." Of course, President Obama describes killing people with missiles from drones or with shoot-to-kill night raids as "bringing them to justice." Neither he nor Allman and Winright mean to imply indictments or prosecutions or anything involving a court of law. Rather they just seem to mean that "revenge" is the wrong term to use when it's their country doing it.

In a similar manner, what the United States or NATO does (even when it is as murderous as the current war on Iraq) is not to be called "genocide," whereas the war making of others can be so designated. This serves to justify Western "interventions" on the understanding that genocide is something worse than war, so using war as a solution to genocide is a price worth paying. In fact numerous events generally deemed "wars" have been worse than other events designated as "genocidal." Both wars and genocides are driven by the arms trade and militarism, and in fact the question of whether something is a war or a genocide critically hinges on the question of *who* did it, rather than *what* was done.

Genocide is defined in Article 2 of the Convention on the Prevention and Punishment of the Crime of Genocide (1948) as "any of the following acts committed with intent to destroy, in whole or in part, a national, ethnical, racial or religious group, as such: killing members of the group; causing serious bodily or mental harm to members of the group; deliberately inflicting on the group conditions of life calculated to bring about its physical destruction in whole or in part; imposing measures intended to prevent births within the group; [and] forcibly transferring children of the group to another group."

This definition has a weakness in its dependence on determining the intentions of governments. But it seems to fit exactly how many top Israelis describe their intentions toward Palestinians.[42] It also fits how many U.S. troops have talked about their intentions during recent U.S. wars that have devastated Middle Eastern countries, and their Muslim, and particularly Sunni Muslim, populations.[43] U.S. wars, sanctions, and bombing campaigns against Iraq have dramatically reduced its overall population, primarily through violent killing, and virtually or entirely eliminated through death and displacement various ethnic and religious minorities.[44] One U.S. veteran, Ethan McCord, explained how his commanders viewed Iraqis:

> "We had a pretty gung-ho commander, who decided that because we were getting hit by IEDs [improvised explosive devices] a lot, there would be a new battalion SOP [standard operating procedure]. He goes, 'If someone in your line gets hit with an IED, 360 rotational fire. You kill every motherfucker on the street.'"[45]

Another way to kill "every motherfucker on the street" is to destroy water supplies, sewage plants, hospitals, and bridges. This the United States did in Iraq most extensively in 1991 and 2003. On the first occasion, a U.S. Air force planning officer justified these criminal acts as no worse than and having no other purpose than economic sanctions: "People say, 'You didn't recognize that it was going to have an effect on water or sewage.' Well, what were we trying to do with sanctions—help out the Iraqi people? No. What we were doing with the attacks on infrastructure was to accelerate the effect of the sanctions."[46]

Yet, somehow none of that is genocide. On the contrary, the supposed need and ability to avert genocide is used as a justification for more U.S. war making in Libya, Syria, and elsewhere.

What can count as a "just cause" gets another big expansion in the course of Allman and Winright's discussion of *jus post bellum*. "The principle aim of a just war," they write, ". . . seeks to put into place at least a 'minimally just state,' one that respects human rights and behaves in a manner that allows it to be seen as legitimate. . . ." What government, I ask you, ever considers the government of its targeted victim to be legitimate? And how often has a war created a minimally just state? Most wars clearly do not do any such thing, so that a reasonable expectation of success seems impossible, and along with it the idea of a Just War.

In the end, "just cause" should be renamed "just because." It suffers from the same weaknesses as "right intention." One can no more reliably predict all the results of a war than one can divine all the intentions of the war makers.

A slideshow used for decades by the U.S. Air Force to persuade new personnel tasked with overseeing and potentially launching nuclear missiles includes a slide that reads: "Just Cause: to avenge or to avert evil; to protect the innocent and restore moral social order. Just Intent: to restore moral order, not expand power; not for pride or revenge." Many dictionaries define both *avenge* and *revenge* as "to take vengeance." How are we to discern whether the Air Force is avenging but not revenging? And how can we challenge its authority when it tells us, in another slide, "Revelation 19:11 Jesus Is The Mighty Warrior"? The same slide show includes demonstrable falsehoods about Hiroshima, and holds up as a moral model a man who used slave labor to build rockets for Nazis (Werner von Braun), but the claims of "Just War" status for nuking people are not actually disprovable.[47]

"Just Cause," by the way, was the U.S. military's name for its 1989 attack on Panama, which it claimed was prompted by an incident that actually occurred months after the plans had been made for the war.[48]

PROPORTIONALITY

An additional non-empirical Just War criterion is that of proportionality. The word appears in every Just War theory and in thousands of mainstream news reports, yet nobody has ever devised a test whereby one can determine whether a war or a particular bombing was "proportional" or not. If I say killing 14 children in order to kill a particular man was disproportional, what's to stop someone else arguing that this particular man needed to be killed to an extent that would have justified killing anywhere up to 16.37 children? Of course, I can point out that most wars kill mostly civilians, so that launching them is an act that guarantees great injustice, but I can't stop someone else claiming that "proportionally" killing 500,000 children is "worth it" in the context of some just cause (as U.S. Secretary of State Madeleine Albright once claimed).[49]

SOME JUST WAR CRITERA ARE NOT POSSIBLE

Some Just War criteria have never been and can never be met. These include:

1. Last Resort
2. Reasonable Prospect of Success
3. Noncombatants Immune from Attack
4. Enemy Soldiers Respected as Human Beings
5. Prisoners of War Treated as Noncombatants

LAST RESORT

It is of course a step in the right direction when a culture moves from Theodore Roosevelt's open desire for a new war for war's sake, to the universal pretense that every war is and must be a last resort. This pretense is so universal now, that the U.S. public simply assumes it without even being told. A scholarly study recently found that the U.S. public believes that whenever the U.S. government proposes a war, it has already exhausted all other possibilities. When a sample group was asked if they supported a particular war, and a second group was asked if they supported that particular war after being told that all alternatives were no good, and a third group was asked if they supported that war even though there were good alternatives, the first two groups registered the same level of support, while support for war dropped off significantly in the third group. This led the researchers to the conclusion that if alternatives are not mentioned, people don't assume they exist— rather, people assume they've already been tried.[50]

There have for years been major efforts in Washington, D.C., to start a war on Iran. Some of the greatest pressure has come in 2007 and 2015. If that war had been started at any point, it would no doubt have been described as a last resort, even though the choice of simply not starting that war has been chosen on numerous occasions. In 2013, the U.S. President told us of the urgent "last resort" need to launch a major bombing campaign on Syria. Then he reversed his decision, largely because of public resistance to it. It turned out the option of *not* bombing Syria was also available.

Imagine an alcoholic who managed every night to consume huge quantities of whiskey and who every morning swore that drinking whiskey had been his very last resort, he'd had no choice at all. Easy to imagine, no doubt. An addict will always justify himself, however nonsensically it has to be done. But imagine a world in which everyone believed him and solemnly said to each other "He really had no other choice. He truly had tried everything else." Not so plausible, is it? Almost unimaginable, in fact. And yet:

It is widely believed that the United States is at war in Syria as a last resort, even though:

- The United States spent years sabotaging UN attempts at peace in Syria.[51]
- The United States dismissed out of hand a Russian peace proposal for Syria in 2012.[52]
- And when the United States claimed a bombing campaign was needed immediately as a "last resort" in 2013 but the U.S. public was wildly opposed, other options were pursued.

In 2015, numerous U.S. Congress Members argued that the nuclear deal with Iran needed to be rejected and Iran attacked as a last resort. No mention was made of Iran's 2003 offer to negotiate away its nuclear program, an offer that had been quickly scorned by the United States.

It is widely believed that the United States is killing people with drones as a last resort, even though in that minority of cases in which the United States knows the names of the people it is aiming for, many (and quite possibly all) of them could have been fairly easily arrested.[53]

It was widely believed that the United States killed Osama bin Laden as a last resort, until those involved admitted that the "kill or capture" policy didn't actually include any capture (arrest) option and that bin Laden had been unarmed when he was killed.[54]

It was widely believed the United States attacked Libya in 2011, overthrew its government, and fueled regional violence as a last resort, even though in March 2011 the African Union had a plan for peace in Libya but was prevented by NATO, through the creation of a "no fly zone" and the initiation of bombing, to travel to Libya to discuss it. In April, the African Union was able to discuss its plan with Libyan leader Muammar Gaddafi, and he expressed his agreement.[55] NATO had obtained UN authorization to protect Libyans alleged to be in danger, but it had no authorization to continue bombing the country or to overthrow the government.

Virtually anyone who works for, and wishes to continue working for, a major U.S. media outlet says the United States attacked Iraq in 2003 as a last resort or sort of meant to, or something, even though:

- The U.S. president had been concocting cockamamie schemes to get a war started.[56]
- The Iraqi government had approached the CIA's Vincent Cannistraro with an offer to let U.S. troops search the entire country.[57]
- The Iraqi government offered to hold internationally monitored elections within two years.[58]
- The Iraqi government made an offer to Bush official Richard Perle to open the whole country to inspections, to turn over a suspect in the 1993 World Trade Center bombing, to help fight terrorism, and to favor U.S. oil companies.[59]
- The Iraqi president offered, in the account that the president of Spain was given by the U.S. president, to simply leave Iraq if he could keep $1 billion.[60]
- The United States always had the option of simply not starting another war.

Most everyone supposes that the United States invaded Afghanistan in 2001 and has stayed there ever since as a series of "last resorts," even though the Taliban repeatedly offered to turn bin Laden over to a third country to stand trial, al Qaeda has had no significant presence in Afghanistan for most of the duration of the war, and withdrawal has been an option at any time.[61]

Many maintain that the United States went to war with Iraq in 1990-1991 as a "last resort," even though the Iraqi government was willing to negotiate withdrawal from Kuwait without war and ultimately offered to simply withdraw from Kuwait within three weeks without conditions. The King of Jordan, the Pope, the President of France, the President of the Soviet Union, and many others urged such a peaceful settlement, but the White House insisted upon its "last resort."[62]

Even setting aside general practices that increase hostility, provide weaponry, and empower militaristic governments, as well as fake negotiations intended to facilitate rather than avoid war, the history of U.S. war making can be traced back through the centuries as a story of an endless series of opportunities for peace carefully avoided at all costs.

Mexico was willing to negotiate the sale of its northern half, but the United States wanted to take it through an act of mass killing. Spain wanted the matter of the *Maine* to go to international arbitration, but the U.S. wanted war and empire. The Soviet Union proposed peace negotiations before the Korean War. The United States sabotaged peace proposals for Vietnam from the Vietnamese, the Soviets, and the French, relentlessly insisting on its "last resort" over any other option, from the day the Gulf of Tonkin incident mandated war despite never having actually occurred.[63]

If you look through enough wars, you'll find nearly identical incidents used on one occasion as the excuse for a war and on another occasion as nothing of the sort. President George W. Bush proposed to U.K. Prime Minister Tony Blair that getting a U2 airplane shot at could get them into a war they wanted.[64] Yet when the Soviet Union shot down a U2 airplane, President Dwight Eisenhower started no war.

Yes, yes, yes, one might reply, hundreds of actual and unjust wars are not last resorts, even though their supporters claim that status for them. But a theoretical Just War would be a last resort. Would it? Would there really be no other option morally equivalent or superior? Allman and Winright quote Pope John Paul II on the "duty to disarm this aggressor if all other means have proven ineffective." But is "disarm" really the equivalent of "bomb or invade"? We've seen wars launched supposedly to disarm, and the result has been more weapons than ever before. What about *ceasing to arm* as one possible method of disarming? What about an international arms embargo? What about economic and other incentives to disarm?

There was no moment when bombing Rwanda would have been a moral "last resort." There was a moment when armed police might have helped, or cutting off a radio signal being used to provoke killings might have helped. There were many moments when unarmed peaceworkers would have helped. There was a moment when demanding accountability for the assassination of the president would have helped. There were three years before that when refraining from arming and funding Ugandan killers would have helped.

"Last resort" claims are usually pretty weak when one imagines traveling back in time to the moment of crisis, but dramatically weaker still if one just imagines traveling back a bit further. Many more people try to justify World War II than World War I, even though one of them could never have happened without the other or without the dumb manner of ending it, which led numerous observers at the time to predict World War II with significant accuracy. If attacking ISIS in Iraq now is somehow a "last resort" it is only because of the war that was escalated in 2003, which couldn't have happened without the earlier Gulf War, which couldn't have happened without arming and supporting Saddam Hussein in the Iran-Iraq war, and so on back through the centuries. Of course unjust causes of crises don't render all new decisions unjust, but they suggest that someone with an idea other than more war should intervene in a destructive cycle of self-justifying crisis generation.

Even in the moment of crisis, is it really as urgent a crisis as war supporters claim? Is a clock really ticking here any more than in torture thought experiments? Allman and Winright suggest this list of alternatives to war that must have been exhausted for war to be a last resort: "smart sanctions, diplomatic efforts, third-party negotiations, or an ultimatum."[65] That's it? This list is to the full list of available alternatives what the National Public Radio show "All Things Considered" is to all things. They ought to rename it "Two Percent of Things Considered." Later, Allman and Winright quote a claim that overthrowing governments is kinder than "containing" them. This argument, the authors maintain, challenges "pacifist and contemporary just war theorists alike." It does? Which option were those two types supposedly favoring? "Containment"? That's not a very peaceful approach and certainly not the only alternative to war.

If a nation were actually attacked and chose to fight back in defense, it would not have the time for sanctions and each of the other options listed. It wouldn't even have time for academic support from Just War theorists. It would just find itself fighting back. The area for Just War theory to work in is, therefore, at least in great part, those wars that are something short of defensive, those wars that are "preemptive," "preventive," "protective," etc.

The first step up from actually defensive is a war launched to prevent an imminent attack. The Obama Administration has, in recent years, redefined "imminent" to mean theoretically possible someday. They then claimed to be murdering with drones only people who constituted "an imminent and continuing threat to the United States." Of course, if it were imminent under the usual definition, it wouldn't be continuing, because it would happen.

Here is a critical passage from the Department of Justice "White Paper" defining "imminent":

"[T]he condition that an operational leader present an 'imminent' threat of violent attack against the United States does not require the United States to have clear evidence that a specific attack on U.S. persons and interests will take place in the immediate future."[66]

The George W. Bush Administration saw things in a similar way. The 2002 U.S. National Security Strategy states: "We recognize that our best defense is a good offense."[67] Of course, this is false, as offensive wars stir up hostility. But it is also admirably honest.

Once we're talking about non-defensive war proposals, about crises in which one has time for sanctions, diplomacy, and ultimatums, one also has time for all sorts of other things. Possibilities include: nonviolent (unarmed) civilian-based defense: announcing the organization of nonviolent resistance to any attempted occupation, global protests and demonstrations, disarmament proposals, unilateral disarmament declarations, gestures of friendship including aid, taking a dispute to arbitration or court, convening a truth and reconciliation commission, restorative dialogues, leadership by example through joining binding treaties or the International Criminal Court or through democratizing the United Nations, civilian diplomacy, cultural collaborations, and creative nonviolence of endless variety.

But what if we imagine an actually defensive war, either the much feared but ridiculously impossible invasion of the United States, or a U.S. war viewed from the other side? Was it just for the Vietnamese to fight back? Was it just for the Iraqis to fight back? Et cetera. (I mean this to include the scenario of an attack on the actual land of the United States, not an attack on, for example, U.S. troops in Syria. As I write, the United States government is threatening to "defend" its troops in Syria should the government of Syria "attack" them.)

The short answer to that question is that if the aggressor would have refrained, no defense would have been needed. Turning resistance to U.S. wars around into justification for further U.S. military spending is too twisted even for a K Street lobbyist.

The slightly longer answer is that it's generally not the proper role for someone born and living in the United States to advise people living under U.S. bombs that they should experiment with nonviolent resistance.

But the right answer is a bit more difficult than either of those. It's an answer that becomes clearer if we look at both foreign invasions and revolutions/civil wars. There are more of the latter to look at, and there are more strong examples to point to. But the purpose of theory, including Anti-Just-War theory, should be to help generate more real-world examples of superior outcomes, such as in the use of nonviolence against foreign invasions.

Studies like Erica Chenoweth's have established that nonviolent resistance to tyranny is far more likely to succeed, and the success far more likely to be lasting, than with violent resistance.[68] So if we look at something like the nonviolent revolution in Tunisia in 2011, we might find that it meets as many criteria as any other situation for a Just War, except that it wasn't a war at all. One wouldn't go back in time and argue for a strategy less likely to succeed but likely to cause a lot more pain and death. Perhaps doing so might constitute a Just War argument. Perhaps a Just War argument could even be made, anachronistically, for a 2011 U.S. "intervention" to bring democracy to Tunisia (apart from the United States' obvious inability to do such a thing, and the guaranteed catastrophe that would have resulted). But once you've done a revolution without all the killing and dying, it can no longer makes sense to propose all the killing and dying—not if a thousand new Geneva Conventions were created, and no matter the imperfections of the nonviolent success.

Despite the relative scarcity of examples thus far of nonviolent resistance to foreign occupation, there are those already beginning to claim a pattern of success. Here's Stephen Zunes:

"Nonviolent resistance has also successfully challenged foreign military occupation. During the first Palestinian intifada in the 1980s, much of the subjugated population effectively became self-governing entities through massive noncooperation and the creation of alternative institutions, forcing Israel to allow for the creation of the Palestine Authority and self-governance for most of the urban areas of the West Bank. Nonviolent resistance in the occupied Western Sahara has forced Morocco to offer an autonomy proposal which—while still falling well short of Morocco's obligation to grant the Sahrawis their right of self-determination—at least acknowledges that the territory is not simply another part of Morocco.

"*In the final years of German occupation of Denmark and Norway during WWII, the Nazis effectively no longer controlled the population. Lithuania, Latvia, and Estonia freed themselves from Soviet occupation through nonviolent resistance prior to the USSR's collapse. In Lebanon, a nation ravaged by war for decades, thirty years of Syrian domination was ended through a large-scale, nonviolent uprising in 2005. And last year, Mariupol became the largest city to be liberated from control by Russian-backed rebels in Ukraine, not by bombings and artillery strikes by the Ukrainian military, but when thousands of unarmed steelworkers marched peacefully into occupied sections of its downtown area and drove out the armed separatists.*"[69]

One might look for potential in numerous examples of resistance to the Nazis, and in German resistance to the French invasion of the Ruhr in 1923, or perhaps in the one-time success of the Philippines and the ongoing success of Ecuador in evicting U.S. military bases, and of course the Gandhian example of booting the British out of India. But the far more numerous examples of nonviolent success over domestic tyranny also provide a guide toward future action.

To be morally right, nonviolent resistance to an actual attack need not appear more likely to succeed than a violent response. It only need appear somewhat close to as likely. Because if it succeeds it will do so with less harm, and its success will be more likely to last.

In the absence of an attack, while claims are being made that a war should be launched as a "last resort," nonviolent solutions need only appear reasonably plausible. Even in that situation, they must be attempted before launching a war can be labeled a "last resort." But because they are infinite in variety and can be tried over and over again, under the same logic, one will never actually reach the point at which attacking another country is a last resort.

If you could achieve that, a moral decision would still require that the imagined benefits of your war outweigh all the damage done by maintaining the institution of war (see the above section on "Preparing For A Just War Is A Greater Injustice Than Any War").

REASONABLE PROSPECT OF SUCCESS.

What about the criterion that holds that a Just War must have a reasonable prospect of success? I don't think any war that meets many of the other Just War criteria can possibly meet this one. When the United States attacks Grenada or the Dominican Republic, it can claim to have achieved a foreseeable success. But there are two problems. First, the success itself stimulates weapons sales and additional wars that are the furthest thing from successes, as well as leaving behind brewing hostility. Second, you can't match up Right Intention, Just Cause, Proportionality, or Last Resort with a devastating attack on a virtually defenseless nation. But when a war becomes less imbalanced, it quickly becomes impossible to predict success with any sort of certainty, or even to define what success would mean. Wars drag on for years and years because ending them is understood as failure, while success is either nonexistent even as a concept or consists of an impossible fantasy never to be realized. Meanwhile the horrors, short-term and long, pile up. Jeanette Rankin said you can no more win a war than you can win a hurricane, that every victory is, in other words, Pyrrhic. Hence the need for the pretense of "last resort." But you can't even pretend that when launching the sort of war in which success can be predicted.

I am, of course, treating war as an observable phenomenon rather than a White House statement. Allman and Winright seem to treat the Iraq war of 2003 as having been won when and because President Bush *said* it was won. Because he declared victory, they describe the Iraq war from that point on as "post-conflict."[70] Everything after the declaration of "mission accomplished" then becomes a non-war or a post-war or, in the view of war pollyannas like Harvard Psychology Professor Stephen Pinker, a civil war. This can serve to move death statistics out of the "war" column and into some other place where they can be avoided, as well as to shift blame onto the people being occupied. But it doesn't alter the predictable, and predicted, reality in which the killing and dying was going to continue until some time after the invaders departed, if they ever do.

NONCOMBATANTS IMMUNE FROM ATTACK

Another impossible criterion is that which holds noncombatants to be immune from attack. In most wars, noncombatants make up the majority of those killed and injured. Anyone launching a war cannot avoid being aware of this. Anyone continuing a war or launching a particular campaign during a war cannot avoid being aware of this. In fact, Just War theorists for centuries have dealt with this problem by playing word games. The Just War notion of "double effect" has much in common with the Orwellian notion of doublethink, in which one believes contradictory things simultaneously. The idea of double effect is that you can know that your bomb might kill a person you're aiming for, while also knowing that it will kill other people, and you can tell yourself that you "intend" to kill the one person, while you are killing all the other people "unintentionally," even though you could save their lives by not dropping the bomb on them.

I should interrupt this text for a quick public service announcement: Do not try "double effect" at home. Do not do your homework while driving your car and then tell the people you run over that you only "intended" to do your homework while getting to class fast, that you knew you might run somebody over but you didn't "intend" it. Nobody's going to buy your reasoning for one simple reason. The technical term for what is wrong with it is that you are committing the fallacy of "bullshitting your ass off." If you persist in this attitude, you may need to look for a career in the U.S. military press offices.

Then there's the problem that arose above when I asked whether Canadians occupying the United States would really have the right to "justly" murder anyone who fought back (and therefore the right to also murder anybody else as "unintentional" and "collateral" damage). David Carroll Cochran, in *Catholic Realism and the Abolition of War*, argues against this idea, making use of a particular understanding of innocence.

Cochran includes among the innocent both civilians and soldiers. Yes, his is a very idiosyncratic use of the term "innocent," driven apparently by the idea that we each must be completely innocent or entirely guilty. But if you can get past the terminology, Cochran has a useful point to make. Cochran does not consider soldiers "innocent" because their side of a war is defensive. He considers them "innocent" on the side of the aggressor as well— and not only those soldiers who quietly regret what they are doing or those who honestly believe the propaganda that would justify their actions. No, even combatants who fully support the war for any variety of reasons are "innocent," in a certain sense, in Cochran's view.

Since I don't think anyone is innocent or believe I have the right to murder anyone who's not innocent, I think a better term would be human. Even soldiers in an aggressive army are human with the right not to be killed. But here's the basis for this claim, whether to innocence or humanity: Cochran points out that it is generally viewed as wrong to kill soldiers who are wounded or surrendering. This, Cochran writes, is because they have done nothing to deserve being slaughtered, although slaughtered they are in the general course of a war.

One idea put forward by war supporters is that in the normal course of war, soldiers are mutually engaged in self-defense against each other, but Cochran points out that the justification of self-defense for individuals outside of war only works when an aggressor has attacked a victim. War is conducted on a very different scale and with very different norms. Soldiers during a war are not expected to try all nonviolent approaches first before resorting to violence and, in fact, routinely kill other soldiers who do not pose any imminent threat. Much killing in historical battles has happened after one side has begun retreating. The United States killed 30,000 retreating Iraqi soldiers during the 1991 Gulf War, for example.

The ultimate fallback justification for the mass-murder of war is that innocents/humans can be slaughtered if the harm done is outweighed by the goals of the war. But such goals are often secret or lied about, and it is the war makers who get to decide whose deaths are outweighed by what goals. (See the problems with Right Intention and Just Cause above.)

Gulf War veteran and terrorist (if that's not redundant) Timothy McVeigh blew up a government building in 1995 and claimed that the deaths that resulted were merely "collateral damage" because killing those people had not been his purpose. The U.S. military plays the same game, the only difference being that it is allowed to get away with it.

Partly the military gets away with it by constantly claiming to have found technological solutions to collateral damage. But, in fact, the latest such ploy—weaponized drones—kills more civilians than it kills people about whom the drone-masters assert any (always unsubstantiated) right to murder.

To call combatants human in analyzing the morality of war is not, in my view, to diminish the moral superiority of refusing to fight. Nor is it to suggest some sort of moral perfection or innocence in the individual lives of soldiers. Nor is it to set aside the Nuremberg standard that requires disobeying illegal orders. Rather, it is to understand that no justification exists for killing soldiers. There might be a justification for otherwise sanctioning their behavior, and—more so—the behavior of those who sent them into war, but not for killing them.

This seems at odds with much of Christian and Western tradition. There may be a bit too much of loving your enemies in it. That's always been a behavior more preferred in word than deed. But surely the inclination to try to think of wars as "last resorts" justified by important "just causes" is built on the understanding that even killing soldiers is undesirable / immoral. After all, the Just War tradition seeks to reimagine war as something that only or primarily kills soldiers. And yet it is this very tradition that strives to avoid war unless it is carefully justified and regulated. Such a tradition, then, should—if it cannot itself be abolished—rid itself of the stark division between the undesirability of killing civilians and the total acceptance of slaughtering combatants without limit—without even counting them, much less telling their stories.

The Just War criterion that forbids killing noncombatants unless you don't "intend" it is often interpreted to support banning particular weapons entirely. This is helpful in as far as it goes, but unhelpful in that it suggests that certain weapons are OK. In 2013 President Obama proposed to kill numerous Syrian men, women, and children with bombs, because some other Syrian people had been killed with chemical weapons in the course of a devastating war that was killing people by the thousands with all variety of weapons, some of them apparently "just" and others "unjust." The fact is that chemical or biological weapons on an actual battlefield, if such a thing can be found, don't target civilians more indiscriminately than bombing towns and cities with "good" weapons does.

The worst weapon we have is the nuclear bomb, and any arguments against using it are appreciated. But Mikhail Gorbachev pointed something out in his recent book, *The New Russia*: Until the United States ends its extreme dominance in "conventional" weapons and foreign bases in its pursuit of global hegemony, abolishing nuclear weapons is very unlikely.[71] Countries want nuclear weapons as a deterrent because they feel threatened. Until the threats end, until White House press secretaries stop saying "All options are on the table," until the arms race is reversed, it will be very difficult to get rid of just one weapon. So, the notion of proper Just Wars carrying on with nukes having been eliminated may not be a real option.

ENEMY SOLDIERS RESPECTED AS HUMAN BEINGS

Perhaps my favorite impossible Just War criterion is that enemy soldiers must be respected as human beings. Allman and Winright explain that Just War theory intends to protect the "enemy neighbor's dignity."[72] To them, apparently, dignity is something that survives death. Your arm might be hanging from a tree, and the rest of you shattered into such small pieces on the ground, so mixed in with pieces of other humans and cattle that they can't be identified—as has been the case with victims of some U.S. missiles—but at least you will have your dignity, because you were blown up respectfully!

Outside of war-justifying theories, Western academia does not generally define respecting someone as including trying to kill them. Typically, respecting someone prevents being rude to them, depriving them of rights, insulting them, discriminating against them, pre-judging them on the basis of stereotypes, condescending to them, or interrupting them when they are talking (which killing them certainly does). There remain cases in which the U.S. government must go to court before it can spy on you. It need do no such thing in order to murder you, along with anybody too nearby you at the time.

Under a common conception of the law, participants in war are given no license to lie, cheat, steal, loot, rape, assault, drive over the speed limit, or fudge their tax returns, but they are allowed to murder. And under Just War theory, you must always respect your "enemy neighbor," even when trying to murder or maim him or her. This is a bizarre deviation from the norms of Western culture. On the television show *Mr. Roger's Neighborhood,* Mr. Rogers almost never tried to lovingly murder or wound his neighbors. Trying to apply the idea of respecting people to the institution of war may be admirable, but that doesn't mean it's possible. It is, fortunately, laughable.

PRISONERS OF WAR TREATED AS NONCOMBATANTS

Finally, there's the criterion that requires that prisoners of war be treated as noncombatants. This one is, indeed, possible in theory, if you ignore the fact that noncombatants are not placed in cages. And one can hold up this criterion as an ideal to be more closely approached. But we have yet to see it accomplished in reality. That is, there hasn't been a war, as far as I know, in which every abuse of every prisoner of war was even intended (in the normal sense) to be "unintended" (in the Just War sense), as is required when abusing noncombatants.

Noncombatants' legal rights are supposed to be respected. The legal rights of prisoners of war are far more extensive than most people imagine. In fact, the new-found popularity of the term "combatants" derives in part from the George W. Bush regime's desire to label prisoners something other than "prisoners," in order to avoid having to respect their rights.

In Michael Haas's book, *George W. Bush, War Criminal? The Bush Administration's Liability for 269 War Crimes*, he lists 175 crimes committed against prisoners, ranging from inhumane treatment to depriving of property, from religious mistreatment to denial of decent burial, from torture to failure to allow prisoners to eat together, from murder to inadequate infirmary, surgical, and hospital care, from involuntary experimentation to inadequate recreational opportunities, from prisoners transferred to countries practicing torture to failure to allow prisoners to elect representatives, from confinement without daylight to failure to advise of right to counsel. Legally, prisoners of war must be provided with care and services never provided to millions of U.S. citizens. Failing to respect the rights of prisoners of war means violating Just War theory. Meanwhile respecting Just War theory motivates the dumping of all of our resources into preparations for wars, thus preventing us from providing decent care and services to prisoners and non-prisoners (ordinary U.S. civilians) alike, while simultaneously influencing (and arming) domestic law enforcement to treat non-prisoners like enemies.

SOME JUST WAR CRITERIA ARE NOT MORAL FACTORS AT ALL

Some just war criteria don't really relate to the morality of a war decision. These include:

1. Publicly declared
2. Waged by legitimate and competent authority

PUBLICLY DECLARED

Imagine if some lesser evil met these criteria. For example, suppose that the U.S. government publicly declared that every Friday it would drown a kitten. Now, suppose that Huck "the Huckster" Higginbotham secretly drowned a kitten every Friday. (He *would*, wouldn't he, given the government's example?)

Which kittens are more drowned, those drowned by the "legitimate authority" after a "public declaration" or those secretly drowned by an "illegitimate" dude with a dirty toilet? Are they not equally drowned? Is not the very idea of a drowned kitten by any other name as morally repugnant? In fact, isn't the greater harm done by the larger and more public power setting a toxic example for others to follow?

And isn't the same true in the case of both a government and someone else doing the same good and beneficial act? Is a kitten rescued from drowning by a government any more or less rescued, except in so far as a positive example is set?

Why does the calculation change when the crime is increased to the mass murder of human beings? Aren't the victims just as dead, wounded, and traumatized regardless of public declarations and the legitimacy of authorities? Or if you imagine a war to be just, isn't it exactly as just either way?

WAGED BY LEGITIMATE AND COMPETENT AUTHORITY

And what is a "legitimate and competent" authority? Allman and Winright suggest that a legitimate and competent authority is a representative one not at fault for any suffering of innocents in its own nation. Of course, that would rule out the U.S. government and most others, as well as depriving governments declared not to meet the standard of their supposed right to defensive Just Wars. In fact, Allman and Winright claim that illegitimacy and incompetence of governments creates the possibility of "just revolution" and "intervention."[73] This may, in fact, be the main function served by these amoral criteria: they allow the theorist to declare certain entities entitled to fight Just Wars, while others deserve to have Just Wars waged against them.

Of course, I would prefer governments to be representative or democratic. Of course, I would prefer everything they do to be transparent. But making the declaration of a war transparent hardly touches the question of its justness or unjustness. A very public announcement and development of plans to commit a single murder would not be more ethical than a secret plan to commit the same crime. Multiplying the number of murders does not change this. And nothing facilitates more government secrecy than launching a war.

These criteria can also be used to suggest that certain authorities are more acceptable than others within a given nation. Allman and Winright point out that the U.S. Constitution requires that Congress, rather than a president, decide on a war. This is helpful only in so far as Congress might be more reluctant to launch wars. A public referendum requirement would be a further step in the same direction. Were Congress to launch wars, however, those wars would be exactly as unjust (in the normal sense) as are presidential wars. Allman and Winright's Just War on Serbia/Kosovo, by the way, was opposed by Congress, and yet they still refer to it as Just. Perhaps they mean that it could have been Just had Congress declared it. And the Constitution makes treaties that the United States is party to the supreme law of the land. One of them, the Kellogg-Briand Pact, bans all war.[74] Another, the UN Charter, bans most wars, including all recent ones. Would a "legitimate" authority wage so many illegal wars and somehow remain "legitimate" should a Just War come along someday? I can't see how. I also can't see what this question has to do with the morality of the wars.

I suspect these criteria derive from the divine rights of kings, and that they are maintained by the common habit of blind subservience to authority—a habit we should leave behind along with war.

THE CRITERIA FOR JUST DRONE MURDERS ARE IMMORAL, INCOHERENT, AND IGNORED

On May 23, 2013, President Barack Obama packed a baker's dozen of lies into a few sentences about his drone murders when he said, "America does not take strikes when we have the ability to capture individual terrorists; our preference is always to detain, interrogate, and prosecute. America cannot take strikes wherever we choose; our actions are bound by consultations with partners, and respect for state sovereignty. America does not take strikes to punish individuals; we act against terrorists who pose a continuing and imminent threat to the American people, and when there are no other governments capable of effectively addressing the threat. And before any strike is taken, there must be near-certainty that no civilians will be killed or injured—the highest standard we can set."[75]

Obama has in fact shifted U.S. policy from lawless imprisonment to murder. We know in detail of numerous cases in which the victim of a drone murder could certainly have been apprehended, but the option of killing was preferred. We know of no cases in which it has been established that a victim could not have been arrested. Obama tossed on the word "prosecute" to suggest that by murdering people and anyone too close to them—and mostly, by the way, people never identified by name or background—he is acting as a global policeman.[76] In fact, we know of no cases where his victims have been charged or indicted, their extradition sought, or a legal case brought against them *in absentia*. There is no evidence of any desire to prosecute them for anything. Obama adds the condition that "no other governments [be] capable of effectively addressing the threat," yet we know of cases in which the local governments of the territories attacked, such as in Yemen, have inquired after the fact, "Why weren't we simply asked to arrest the person?"[77]

Obama's supposed respect for state sovereignty relies on the idea that vicious and antidemocratic governments and exiled dictators can grant him the legal right to blow up men, women, and children in certain parts of the globe. This is actually to engage in a conspiracy to violate state sovereignty, a concept he conveniently has no use for in certain states, like Libya or Syria. "Consultations with partners" has never been a valid criminal defense.

Obama's "near-certainty that no civilians will be killed or injured" is a disgusting insult to the hundreds and thousands of people he kills, most of whom he has not identified, many of whom he has labeled "combatants" because they are male, and many of whom are civilian by any definition, including numerous children and grandparents and attendees of weddings and rescuers of the wounded and those seeking to bury the dead.[78]

There is no such thing as a "continuing and imminent threat to the American people." A threat is either imminent or continuing, but let's assume it can be both, that it is imminent and just goes on and on being imminent. There is not a single example of a U.S. drone murder in which the victim has been shown to have constituted an imminent threat to the people of the United States. In the drone propaganda film *Eye in the Sky* a fantasy is invented in which the victims actually *are* an imminent threat to others. But even then, in a scenario that has never happened and will almost certainly never happen, they are not a threat to the United States or even to its imperial forces.

President Obama's self-imposed criteria for Just Drone Murder (which is surely what they are) have no legal status. They serve to create acceptance for drone murders in the same way that traditional Just War theory seeks to create acceptance of other types of wars. Obama's criteria suffer from the same moral failings and contradictions as the very similar criteria discussed above. The fact that he almost entirely ignores them does not excuse them; it just means that they are serving as cover for something even worse than what they purport to allow.

WHY DO ETHICS CLASSES FANTASIZE ABOUT MURDER SO MUCH?

Why does U.S. culture have such an interest in finding justifications for war? Because it is so dominated by the war machine, by its ideology and by its funding of cultural products.

Quoth Eisenhower over 50 years ago:

> "*This conjunction of an immense military establishment and a large arms industry is new in the American experience. The total influence—economic, political, even spiritual— is felt in every city, every State house, every office of the Federal government.*"[79]

At a post-screening discussion where I questioned the director of *Eye in the Sky* about the disconnect between his drone-kill movie and reality, he launched into a bunch of thought-experiment stuff of the sort I've tried to avoid since finishing my master's in philosophy.[80] Mostly I've avoided hanging out with torture supporters.

Consequentialism, the idea that we should base our actions on the good or bad of the expected consequences, has always been very troubling to philosophy professors, possibly because of some of these reasons:

- It leaves ethics up to humans without any sort of pseudo-divine guidance.
- It means otherwise brilliant people like Immanuel Kant were quite wrong.
- Concluding that consequentialism is the way to go would eliminate the entire academic discipline of debating what is the way to go.

One way to supposedly knock down consequentialism is to propose that if torturing one child could somehow provide pleasure to a million people you would have to do it. But this is simplistic in the extreme. The pain of torture is far greater than the supposed pleasure of watching it. More significantly, this calculation assumes that two minutes after the action in question the world will cease to exist. In a world that continues to exist, significant harm can be expected from the act of encouraging a million people to enjoy watching torture—why in the world would we expect them to stop at one instance of it? And what of the fear that would be instilled in billions of children and their loved ones by a power structure that maintained the right to grab children and torture them? These consequences are, together with the one child's suffering, exactly what make the supposed non-consequentialist object to the horror of the torture, and they are just that: consequences.

A more typical argument against consequentialism is even less persuasive, because it assumes the possession of impossible knowledge, in addition to ignoring medium- and long-term consequences. Such are the ticking time bomb scenarios and the trolley problems that obsess legions of academics across and beyond the United States, and which contribute to the acceptance of "collateral damage" by the U.S. military and the people who fund it. Wikipedia notes something critical about the ticking-time-bomb stories, while dismissing the point as irrelevant:

> "As a thought experiment, there is no need that the scenario be plausible; it need only serve to highlight ethical considerations."[81]

Hmm. How about ethically considering the consequences of filling people's minds and television dramas with scenarios that are not plausible? Television crime dramas have been shown to shape people's political views on crime. Shows like "24" pretend that ticking time-bomb scenarios, in which torture will save many lives, are everyday occurrences. In fact, they only exist and are only likely to ever exist, in fantasy.

In reality, one never has the knowledge that an individual knows how to stop a bomb, that the bomb will soon go off if not stopped, and that the best way to get the truth out of the individual is torture. Torture usually elicits falsehoods or nothing, and no scenario is more likely to do that than one in which the torture victim need only endure a short amount of time in order to accomplish his or her goal.

In reality, U.S. drone kills do not target people who are about to blow up others in the United States or elsewhere, or people who cannot be arrested, or even for the most part people who have been identified by name. But in movie fantasies and public imagination, that is what is going on. When I objected about this to the director of *Eye in the Sky* he launched into a number of trolley problems.

Would you pull a switch to send a trolley onto a track to kill one person, to avoid leaving it on a track where it would kill five people? Would you push a fat man onto the track to die, to save five people? *Et cetera.* In reality you are never going to find yourself in such a situation or its equivalent. How could you know with any certainty what would happen in each case, including that the fat man but not yourself, and not only the two of you together, would stop the trolley?

This nonsense seems harmless because we're not considering actually setting up trolley tracks that we tie people to and push people onto. But the moral dilemma of *Eye in the Sky* is whether to kill people before they can kill more people, even if another and innocent person might be killed as well. The lesson to be drawn is the moral logic of "collateral damage." That leads straight to the CNN moderator asking "Could you order airstrikes that would kill innocent children, not scores but hundreds and thousands. Could you wage war as a commander in chief?"

Do you have the manly resolve to enjoy that thrill of power? If you don't, you can always become an ethics professor and experience it vicariously, fantasizing about which groups of people you would kill and save based on your "intuitions" versus your "calculations." I don't think our professors actually want to rush out and kill people or even order others to do so. But many of them want to vote for politicians who do so. Many of them want to pay taxes for it. Many of them want to tell pollsters that they approve of the President running his finger down a list of men, women, and children on Tuesdays and sagely picking which ones to have murdered.[82]

By the circular reasoning of ethicists, the fact that a culture comes to accept "collateral damage" and, for that matter, non-collateral "damage" means that such acceptance is "true" and must be propped up with some sort of argument.

Let's look at a pair of so-called "case studies" in Allman's book *Who Would Jesus Kill?* In "Case 1" we are told: "During a just war you discover that your enemy has a munitions factory located in a city. The only way to destroy the factory is through a series of missile launches, but the missiles are not 100 percent accurate and some will probably hit a nearby nursing home and apartment complex, thus killing and injuring civilians. Do you launch the missiles?" The authors offer some variations on this theme, but no answers.

Here are my questions:

1. Who identified the factory, and had he or she recently had oral sex? Those may seem irrelevant points to you, but a popular 1997 film called *Wag the Dog* was made on this theme, and there's a shrine in Sudan to worship and honor it. In 1998 President Bill Clinton bombed a pharmaceutical factory in Sudan, depriving many people of much needed medicine, after he falsely claimed it was a chemical weapons factory. Clinton ordered the attack at a time when he had an interest in distracting the media from a ridiculous scandal surrounding his having had oral sex with a White House intern.[83]

2. Why in the world is there only one way to destroy the supposed munitions factory? Can a peace agreement not shut down that munitions factory along with an equivalent munitions factory in the nation proposing the bombing?

3. Most U.S. enemies have U.S.-made weapons. Should the United States be bombing munitions factories in the United States?

4. Can the Just Munitions Factory Bomber be asked to commit to not selling similar munitions to that nation and its

customers for at least, say, 60 days after bombing the factory and killing the civilians?

5. Wouldn't a better thought experiment for people who are not president of the United States be this: How can we organize and apply enough influence on our government so that it stops bombing people?

Here's "Case 2": "During a military campaign in Afghanistan, you discover a cell of ten to fifteen terrorists is operating in a remote town (population ten thousand) that is only accessible by a bridge over a large river. The only way you can ensure the capture of these terrorists is to bomb the bridge and trap them in the town and then send in commandos by air drop. Even if the mission is a success, however, the civilians in the town will be cut off from all food, medicine, and fuel for the entire winter, and many will die, starving or freezing to death. If bombed, the bridge will take months to rebuild. Relocating the entire town is not an option, nor is providing the innocent civilians with food, fuel, and medical supplies for the entire winter. Do you carry out the mission?"

Again, I have questions rather than answers:

1. Does such a one-bridge town actually exist on the real earth?

2. Who are the "terrorists" terrorizing? Armed foreign occupiers of their country, or someone else? Because ending the armed foreign occupation of their country would be an option in the former case. If the "terrorists" are terrorizing locals, then there should be local support for arresting them (not "capturing" them; they are not subhuman animals). An assumption that the locals will not help arrest the "terrorists" should make the Just Warrior stop and wonder why.

3. If the "terrorists" are terrorizing people outside the town, don't they have to either cross the bridge to do so or communicate remotely with others? Can't those communications be blocked or intercepted? Can't that bridge be blocked by the "commandos" rather than blown up?

4. If the "terrorists" are terrorizing local people, why not drop, instead of bombs or commandos: food, medicine, money, information on the "terrorists'" crimes, and offers to discuss collaboration in arresting them?

5. Why is relocating or feeding a small town declared not to be an option? This has recently been done by the government of Syria. Such an expense is a drop in the bucket to the U.S. military, which has wiped out and relocated towns for far less "Just" purposes, even relocating the entire populations of parts of the Philippines and Hawaii, of Puerto Rican and the Aleutian islands, of Pacific atolls including (it's not just a bathing suit but a celebration of nuclear bombs) Bikini, of parts of Okinawa, of Thule in Greenland and (with the British) of the entire island of Diego Garcia.[84]

6. While it might not be as thrilling as contemplating a reassuring pretext for mass murder, wouldn't a more useful question be: What do those 10,000 people want? How can I help them develop local agriculture? Would they like me to build them a second bridge, perhaps designed by a prize-winning architect, for some 0.000000001% of what the U.S. military is about to blow on an inane and immoral operation? And if those 10,000 people do not want to support a fair and just request from me regarding arrests or extraditions, why don't they?

IF ALL JUST WAR CRITERIA WERE MET WAR STILL WOULDN'T BE JUST

I dare to hope that perhaps some of you now share (if you didn't already) my opinion that reviewing Just War criteria helps support war abolition by exposing how irredeemably unjust war is.

If every immeasurable and impossible and amoral Just War criterion were (impossibly) met, a war still would not be justified. There are too many damaging consequences that Just War theory does not consider. Wars generate new enemies and grievances, fuel future violence, strip away civil liberties, empower war profiteers, destroy the natural environment, deprive us of resources needed for truly just causes, spread racism and bigotry, and teach violence and hatred. And planning for the possibility of war leads to war after war after war, none of them just—none of them even close to just.

If you don't accept this conclusion, perhaps you will, following my review of the top candidates for Actual Just War below. If you do now or later accept my conclusion, then it follows that Just War has the same status as Just Rape or Just Child Abuse or Just Slavery or any other such product of doublethink.

JUST WAR THEORISTS DO NOT SPOT NEW UNJUST WARS ANY FASTER THAN ANYONE ELSE

I think Just War theorists can provide a certain moral aspect to pointing out violations of treaty obligations in the treatment of prisoners of war. Or they can give a certain moral sanction to wars they approve of. But when it comes to raising powerful and decisive voices against blatantly unjust wars (if that's not redundant), they seem to lag a ways behind both war abolitionists and many ordinary people lacking any particular theory for or against war in general.

Allman and Winright claim to have "raised questions—before, during, and now 'after'—about the justice of" the ongoing U.S. wars on Afghanistan and Iraq. As evidence for this they cite statements they published in 2007 and 2008.[85] I hope they did more than "raise questions," and I hope they did it some five to seven years earlier than the sources they cite. Allman and Winright cite Michael Walzer as a prominent Just War theorist, claiming that his arguments years prior to the Pentagon's current wars "ring prophetic."[86] But here's what Michael Walzer wrote in the *New York Times* on March 7, 2003, just prior to Washington's "Shock and Awe" terrorist assault on Baghdad. Walzer argued that the only alternative to a major war on Iraq was a little war that would call on the United States to intensify the long-standing sanctions and bombings and declare a "no fly zone" to encompass all of Iraq. Walzer even explicitly blamed France for suggesting that a war should be a "last resort."[87]

But why shouldn't the big new war have been a last resort? Don't Just War theorists who quote Michael Walzer usually tell us that all wars should be "last resorts"? Shouldn't even the "little war" (his phrase) that Walzer pushed as an alternative to a big war have been a last resort after trying everything else, such as . . . oh, I don't know . . . *not* waging war?

One doesn't actually need a last resort or even a first resort means of forcing a country to give up nonexistent weapons, or of compelling a country to bow before total foreign domination. I mean, not if we're still making references to morality. Walzer's impatience with insistence on the "last resort" criteria, however, was typical of most neoliberal hawks who had never directly studied Just War theory. Walzer's intense study of it seems to have done him not the slightest good in this regard.

The same failure seems typical of "progressive" Congress members and activists who claim to take an interest in Just War theory without actually publishing books on it. Take the example of my former U.S. Congressman from here in Virginia, Tom Perriello, a Democrat, Catholic, and Just-War "progressive." He voted for every war dollar he could get his hands on while in Congress. We peace activists met with him, and he told us that he thought the war in Afghanistan was doing a lot of good. After he lost a bid for reelection, Perriello became president of the Center for American Progress Action Fund, a pro-war, Lockheed Martin-funded, Democratic Party-leaning, "progressive" organization.[88] He's also a founder of Avaaz, an online civic action group that has pushed for U.S. wars in Libya and Syria. Perriello has used Just War arguments to push for those same wars.[89] Perriello holds up the Persian Gulf War, Kosovo, and Libya as just wars, and he wants more of them. He explains his position in Just War terms, except that he is more eager than some Just War theorists to claim actual wars as "Just," as well as to explicitly state that Just Wars need not be legal:[90]

> "While the UN Security Council remains the most formal standard for international legitimacy, many nations consider it less representative than regional bodies and less responsive than reality sometimes demands. Today, the United States has a range of options to validate such uses of military might for humanitarian concerns."

I'll address some of Perriello's Just Wars, and others, below.

A JUST-WAR OCCUPATION OF A CONQUERED COUNTRY IS NOT JUST

One of the things we need most urgently is faster rejection of new wars. This is because it has proven vastly more difficult to end wars once they've begun than to prevent them in the first place. One of the reasons it's hard to end them is that at least some Just War theorists, and those who think like them, want unjust wars continued in an effort to make them more just—and the more unjustly they began, the more these theorists want them continued.

> "The United States has a post bellum responsibility," write Allman and Winright, "to provide security until it has accomplished the mission(s) it claimed as its objective(s). Furthermore, considering that bringing democracy and regime change are dubious just causes from an ad bellum

perspective in the first place, such causes only make the post bellum *responsibilities that much greater."*[91]

In the above passage, the authors are referring to the current U.S. war on Iraq in particular. By "post bellum" or "after war" they mean "after the government is overthrown." Not only is overthrowing a government "dubious" as a "just cause," but it is illegal. It also doesn't equate to the ending of a war. The "post war" phase in Allman and Winright's theorizing is simply the continuation of the war after the government has been overthrown but before the population has been pacified or eliminated. Overthrowing the government of Iraq and "bringing democracy" were also not the primary causes proclaimed at the start of the war. Rulers like Tony Blair who felt obliged to feign compliance with laws claimed that overthrow was not a goal, that ridding Iraq of weapons was. Ridding Iraq of its nonexistent weapons was also overwhelmingly the cause articulated by the Bush government. In fact, Deputy so-called Defense Secretary Paul Wolfowitz said that when the Bush White House was trying to concoct plausible justifications for the war before beginning it, removing "weapons of mass destruction" was the one excuse that everyone could agree on, so that was the one they pushed publicly.[92]

One page before the passage quoted above, Allman and Winright list as causes for the Iraq war: eliminating weapons, liberating people, enforcing UN sanctions, eradicating a safe haven for global terrorists, and bringing democracy and stability to the Middle East. (There was no mention of avenging Bush's daddy or obeying God's calling.) Now, we know that the weapons did not exist, and that there was never any good reason to imagine they did.[93] We know that the UN rejected the idea that this war would somehow be enforcing its resolutions.[94] We know that there was no safe haven for global terrorists and that there was never any good reason to think there was.[95] And we know that U.S. and British government experts predicted quite accurately that the result of attacking Iraq would be instability, not stable democracy in the Middle East.[96] Nonetheless, Allman and Winright declare that it would violate Just War principles to end the war before the "just causes" are accomplished. In the meantime, they point out, Iraq remains in a state of "anarchy."

But how do you accomplish the removal of nonexistent weapons? How do you liberate people from someone you've already killed? How do you enforce UN resolutions that in no way permit your so enforcing them and that are not being violated and arguably were not being violated? How do you eradicate a previously nonexistent safe haven for terrorists through engaging in more of what has actually now created one? And how can you bring about stability through the continuation of the kind of military aggression that foments instability? Other parts of the world are also unstable and undemocratic. Why is there not a duty to kill lots of people in a futile effort to improve those other places as well? Why is it relevant that you created this particular disaster? Why does that give you the responsibility to keep making it even worse by trying to fix it?

Allman and Winright invoke, without irony, the Pottery Barn rule. Prior to the invasion of Iraq, Secretary of State Colin Powell reportedly told President Bush "You are going to be the proud owner of 25 million people. You will own all their hopes, aspirations, and problems. You'll own it all." According to investigative reporter and author Bob Woodward, "Powell and Deputy Secretary of State Richard Armitage called this the Pottery Barn rule: You break it, you own it." Senator John Kerry cited the rule when running for president, and it was and is widely accepted as legitimate by Republican and Democratic politicians in Washington, D.C.

The Pottery Barn is a store that has no such rule, at least not for accidents. It's illegal in many states in the United States to have such a rule, except for cases of gross negligence and willful destruction. That description, of course, fits the invasion of Iraq to a T. But how does one manage to own people? It's striking that Powell, an African American, some of whose ancestors were owned as slaves in Jamaica, told the president he would own people, specifically dark-skinned people against whom many Americans held some (now ever growing) degree of prejudice.

If the United States and its fig-leaf "coalition" of minor contingents from other nations had pulled out of Iraq when George W. Bush declared "mission accomplished" in a flight suit on an aircraft carrier in San Diego Harbor on May 1, 2003, and not disbanded the Iraqi military, not laid siege to towns and neighborhoods, not inflamed ethnic tensions, not prevented Iraqis from working to repair the damage, not driven millions of Iraqis out of their homes, not tortured future ISIS leaders in prison camps, not kicked in so many doors to scream the equivalent of "suck on this," etc., then the result would not have been ideal, but it almost certainly would have involved less misery than what was actually done and is still being done, following the Pottery Barn rule.

If someone were to break into your house and smash your furniture and rape your daughter and kill your uncle and release nuclear radiation in your dining room, would you believe that person had a moral obligation to stay and spend the night, or a moral obligation to turn himself in at the nearest police station? Which would show you more respect? Which would be closer to that person loving his enemy, and which, on the other hand, would be closer to Allman and Winright's goal, as I would characterize it, of more competently occupying your enemy?

Allman and Winright argue that they favor punishment for the crime of aggression, but it's not clear whether they apply this to the U.S. war on Iraq, which they also want continued until impossible goals are reached. They write that they favor reparations payments, and they do explicitly apply this to Iraq, and yet they want reparations made without ending the ongoing war and occupation.

They describe the just and stable and democratic country that must be created by an unjust violent foreign occupation before that occupation can justly be ended. The local military and police are to be kept separate from each other—and somehow a foreign military acting as a police force is to make that happen. They paint a picture of good policing and good governance that the United States has proven itself incapable of at home, much less possessing the ability to impose by force on others. The idea of attempting it by example rather than by force does not seem to have been considered.

JUST WAR THEORY OPENS THE DOOR TO PRO-WAR THEORY

From the position of a war abolitionist like me to the position of someone openly and honestly advocating for war for the profits of weapons makers, the first big step is to accept the concept of Just War theory. The next step is to accept the theory of Just Occupation, aka *post bellum* Just War Making. Continuing an occupation until it "succeeds," just like prolonging an occupation in order to "support the troops," is an open door to endless war.

The next big step is to accept the idea that even unjust wars are justified because they serve some sort of higher long-term justice. This is the position of a truly inane book by Ian Morris called *War: What Is It Good For? Conflict and Progress of Civilization from Primates to Robots*. In Morris' mythology, war brings empire, and empire brings peace. In reality, larger nations and empires are not always created by wars, and are not generally more peaceful. And the wars they wage have a tendency to sow chaos and violence around the world.

The final step from supporting unjust wars for an imaginary greater good to supporting them for open greed and sadism is not a huge one. While those who have taken what I'm calling the first step do not of course harbor some secret intention to take additional ones, I think we should resist even the first step down this path, as each step supports, to some degree, a march towards avoidable destruction and chaos.

WE CAN END WAR WITHOUT WAITING FOR JESUS

"War is, in our view," write Allman and Winright, "unfortunately, something that happens due to the lingering presence of sin in this transitional time between Christ's resurrection and the consummation of the reign of God with Christ's return."[97]

I take this to mean that Allman and Winright would not mind seeing war abolished, would like to see war abolished. But they seem to believe that abolishing war is not a job for "mere" humans. War simply must exist because there is sin or evil in the world, the evil of whoever you're making war against, even if their evil is not as evil as the war itself. And that's just the way it must be until the biblical Apocalypse brings about the prophesized end of the world.

I don't mean to belittle beliefs that people hold dear, although I think we should break the habit of holding beliefs dear and start holding beliefs only up to the point that we encounter better ones. But the idea of Christ's return is, from a modern secular perspective, as well as the perspective of believers in other religions, an ancient fairytale—no more and no less, and no hostility intended. There is great value in many ancient fairytales when properly understood. Whether you "believe in" Christ's return or not, we ought to all be able to agree that it is a matter of blind faith rather than proven truth. And that same sort of faith, I would point out, is what allows people to imagine that a "legitimate authority" knows better than they do when to launch a campaign of mass-murder. I find waiting for the rebirth of an ancient figure so that he can abolish war

disempowering and deeply antidemocratic. And I find the habits of thought it encourages quite dangerous.

Then there's the problem that millions, though by no means all, believers in a world-ending Second Coming believe that Israel's wars will help speed it along. Unfortunately, this has provided a quasi-moral argument for tolerating or supporting Israel's wars and giving Israel billions of dollars in free weapons every year, which incidentally boosts weapons sales across the rest of the region. One prominent proponent of bringing about the end of the world through Israeli militarism, Frank Amedia, maintains that electing Donald Trump president is the first step. How does he know this? "The Lord" spoke to him.[98]

Of course many of our best peace activists and war abolitionists are Catholic or members of other religions. Without peace-making Catholics and Quakers and others, the U.S. peace movement would be shattered, and my own understanding of peace advocacy would be deeply impoverished. Of course, that's all true, but all of that good *could* be done without supporting doctrines that disempower us and train us in dangerous habits of thought.

"All Catholics are called to be peacemakers," write Allman and Winright, "to pray for peace and work toward the abolition of war. This should be a commitment not only of Catholic pacifists—who believe that all war and violence are immoral—but also of Catholics who think that armed force is sometimes morally justified."[99]

Now, why exactly should one work to abolish something that is sometimes morally justified? If I believed something was sometimes morally justified, there would be nothing in the world you could do to get me to work for its abolition. "Morally justified" does not typically mean, and Allman and Winright clearly do not mean by it "permissible if you don't have anything better." On the contrary, it means "required if you want to cause the most good and avoid the most evil." But, I suppose, one can write books striving to justify wars (even if what is "intended" is only limiting wars) while praying for the end of war. That can make sense, I guess, if the praying is technically for a bank shot, if you're praying, not for yourself to take part in an abolition movement and succeed, but for Jesus to return, after which war will be ended without human effort.

But, in the absence of coming to "believe in" Jesus, it's not clear what I am to do with any of this as an argument against moving ahead with war abolition by the creatures who invented war in the first place: human beings.

In April 2016, Pope Francis sent a message to the peace-building conference in Rome. He stated that "... the ultimate and most deeply worthy goal of human beings and of the human community is the abolition of war."[100] He mentioned no need to wait for Jesus, or for Godot for that matter. The meeting was announced with a statement from its organizers that the "just war" idea "can no longer claim center stage as *the* Christian approach to war and peace."[101]

Unfortunately, this announcement was not of a total break from the church's traditional acceptance of war, but it did suggest an interest in moving in a better direction. Most significantly, it clearly called for a total rejection of the phrase "Just War":

> *"Emphasizing the need to work for a just peace, the Church is moving away from the acceptability of calling war 'just.' While clear ethical criteria are necessary for addressing egregious attacks or threats in a violent world, moral theologians and ethicists should no longer refer to such criteria as the 'just war theory,' because that language undermines the moral imperative to develop tools and capacity for nonviolent conflict."* Organizers want a "new articulation of Catholic teaching on war and peace, including explicit rejection of 'just war' language."[102]

A statement that emerged from the meeting, included these lines: "We believe that there is no 'just war.' Too often the 'just war theory' has been used to endorse rather than prevent or limit war. Suggesting that a 'just war' is possible also undermines the moral imperative to develop tools and capacities for nonviolent transformation of conflict." It called on the Catholic church to "no longer use or teach 'just war theory'; continue advocating for the abolition of war and nuclear weapons."[103]

On August 26, 2016, Pope Francis announced the theme of his January 1, 2017, World Day of Peace speech. The announcement included these words: "[N]on-violence, understood as a political method, can constitute a realistic way to overcome armed conflicts. In this perspective, it becomes important to increasingly recognize not the right of force but the force of right."[104]

With regard to the question of waiting for Jesus before abolishing war, Pope Paul VI in 1965 wrote these words as part of the "Pastoral Constitution of the Church in the Modern World," and they are quoted in the "Catechism of the Catholic Church"[105]: "Insofar as men are sinful, the threat of war hangs over them, and hang over them it will until the return of Christ. But insofar as men vanquish sin by a union of love, they will vanquish violence as well and make these words come true: 'They shall turn their swords into plough-shares, and their spears into sickles. Nation shall not lift up sword against nation, neither shall they learn war any more' (Isaiah 2:4)."[106] This passage seems to hedge all bets. In one sense we can't go ahead and abolish war, but in another sense we can. Let's choose the latter.

WHO WOULD THE GOOD SAMARITAN CARPET BOMB?

Allman and Winright imagine that those who disagree with them are "pacifists—who believe that all war and violence are immoral." But why in the world would someone who believed organized mass murder was immoral have to also believe that using violence in defending himself against a mugger would always be immoral? The two situations have almost nothing in common. War is an institution that must be planned for, invested in, and organized. It involves people ordering other people to do horrible things for obscure reasons. It harms mostly people who had nothing to do with those obscure reasons. It creates cycles of blowback. There are always superior alternatives available.

Opposing "all violence" is a different question entirely. As a war abolitionist I'll be called "a pacifist," but not for any sensible reason. Must I oppose restraining a mentally ill and violent individual? Of course there are nonviolent options available in small-scale human conflicts to a far, far greater extent than is commonly supposed. But to argue that they are always available in every single instance would be a different book from this one, in which I am making an argument about war and only about war.

Allman and Winright try to enlist Jesus Christ on the side of Just Warriors by asking what Jesus would have suggested had the Good Samaritan come upon the mugging victim while he was still being mugged.[107] I don't know about Jesus, but I would say the Samaritan should have tried to stop the violence without joining in it if possible, and should not have joined in it if that appeared likely to only increase the harm, but that he perhaps could have used limited violence in the unlikely event that it was necessary and only to the extent necessary. The Samaritan had wealth to share, he had kindness, he had his voice. The idea that all he had to work with was violence is misguided. But even more misguided is the idea that a roadside robbery is the same thing as a war.

Allman and Winright then ask what a Good Samaritan should have done if faced with a massacre of hundreds of people in an African village. Then they ask what a Good Samaritan should have done. Well, he should not have bombed the village to save it. He should not have massacred the perpetrators and their village the next day to "send a message." He should not have armed the victims to distribute some of the suffering to the other side and escalate the conflict. He should not have escalated a war. He should, of course, as Allman and Winright agree, have taken numerous steps to avoid the conflict in the first place. And if it arrived he should have employed his special skills and resources to attempt to negotiate a resolution to the conflict. He should have tried engaging the services of international nonviolent peaceworkers and journalists, whose presence has prevented massacres.[108] He should have tried evacuation. And, in the unlikely event of nonviolent alternatives being exhausted, he could perhaps have tried the deterrence of armed guards deployed in combination with these other approaches. But for nonviolent alternatives to be exhausted requires a failure of imagination and ingenuity. There is no reason to suppose that alternatives cannot be found in a small scale conflict any more than in a large scale war, though of course the damage done by failing to find them is less.

Picking the best possible nonviolent solutions to attempt requires knowing more about the situation. When the story is simply that evil irrational people are coming to slaughter villagers for no reason, it's harder to know where to start than if we know the actual thinking of the people involved, their grievances, and their (obviously non-just) motivations. An outside power capable of dropping in a multi-billion-dollar force to slaughter the slaughterers is also perfectly capable of dropping in a construction crew to build them their preferred place of worship to replace one that was burned, or of dropping in 10,000 shiny new tractors with ribbons on them together with irrigation equipment, seed, etc., or of meeting them on a dirt road while paving it, or of parachuting in an entire state fair with food, games, rides, and music. Part of what limits the imagination, I think, is resistance to recognizing exactly how much money it costs to kill people. Once you start thinking in those terms, it becomes possible to ask not merely "Do you think dropping some flyers will help?" but also, "Do you think dropping enough food for a year will help?" or "Do you think it would help to put the village in the middle of a lake with free jet ski rides to it and a free hotel room for anyone who comes unarmed?" My point is not that this is likely to be the solution, but that there are millions of solutions that can be explored based on the actual circumstances—and that they must be explored before anything can be called a last resort.

The African village thought experiment is in essence the same as the role played by "Rwanda" in the West's theory of "humanitarian war." I'll address that case below, along with others. But I must address first the Mother of All Modern Just War Mythologies: World War II.

WORLD WAR TWO WAS NOT JUST

World War II is often called "the good war," and has been since the U.S. war on Vietnam to which it was then contrasted. World War II so dominates U.S. and therefore Western entertainment and education, that "good" often comes to mean something more than "just." The winner of the 2016 "Miss Italy" beauty pageant got herself into a bit of a scandal by declaring that she would have liked to live through World War II. While she was mocked, she was clearly not alone. Many would like to be part of something widely depicted as noble, heroic, and exciting. Should they actually find a time machine, I recommend they read the statements of some actual WWII veterans and survivors before they head back to join the fun.[109] For purposes of this book, however, I am going to look only at the claim that WWII was morally just.

No matter how many years one writes books, does interviews, publishes columns, and speaks at events, it remains virtually impossible to make it out the door of an event in the United States at which you've advocated abolishing war without somebody hitting you with the what-about-the-good-war question. This belief that there was a good war 75 years ago is a large part of what moves the U.S. public to tolerate dumping a trillion dollars a year into preparing in case there's a good war next year,[110] even in the face of so many dozens of wars during the past 70 years on which there's general consensus that they were not good. Without rich, well-established myths about World War II, current propaganda about Russia or Syria or Iraq or China would sound as crazy to most people as it sounds to me. And of course the funding generated by the Good War legend leads to more bad wars, rather than preventing them. I've written on this topic at great length in many articles and books, especially *War Is A Lie*.[111] But I'll offer here a few key points that ought to at least place a few seeds of doubt in the minds of most U.S. supporters of WWII as a Just War.

Allman and Winright, again, are not very forthcoming with their list of Just Wars, but they do mention in passing numerous unjust elements of the U.S. role in WWII, including U.S. and U.K. efforts to wipe out the populations of German cities[112] and the insistence on unconditional surrenders.[113] However, they also suggest that they may believe this war was justly engaged in, unjustly conducted, and justly followed through on via the Marshall Plan, etc.[114] I'm not sure Germany's role as host of U.S. troops, weapons, and communications stations, and as collaborator in unjust U.S. wars over the years is included in the calculation.

Here are what I think of as the top 12 reasons the Good War wasn't good/just.

1. World War II could not have happened without World War I, without the stupid manner of starting World War I and the even stupider manner of ending World War I which led numerous wise people to predict World War II on the spot, or without Wall Street's funding of Nazi Germany for decades (as preferable to communists), or without the arms race and numerous bad decisions that do not need to be repeated in the future.

2. The U.S. government was not hit with a surprise attack. President Franklin Roosevelt had quietly promised Churchill that the United States would work hard to provoke Japan into staging an attack. FDR knew the attack was coming, and initially drafted a declaration of war against both Germany and Japan on the evening of Pearl Harbor. Prior to Pearl Harbor, FDR had built up bases in the U.S. and multiple oceans, traded weapons to the Brits for bases, started the draft, created a list of every Japanese American person in the country, provided planes, trainers, and pilots to China, imposed harsh sanctions on Japan, and advised the U.S. military that a war with Japan was beginning. He told his top advisers he expected an attack on December 1st, which was six days off. Here's an entry in Secretary of War Henry Stimson's diary following a November 25, 1941, White House meeting: "The

President said the Japanese were notorious for making an attack without warning and stated that we might be attacked, say next Monday, for example."

3. The war was not humanitarian and was not even marketed as such until after it was over. There was no poster asking you to help Uncle Sam save the Jews. A ship of Jewish refugees from Germany was chased away from Miami by the Coast Guard. The U.S. and other nations refused to accept Jewish refugees, and the majority of the U.S. public supported that position. Peace groups that questioned Prime Minister Winston Churchill and his foreign secretary about shipping Jews out of Germany to save them were told that, while Hitler might very well agree to the plan, it would be too much trouble and require too many ships. The U.S. engaged in no diplomatic or military effort to save the victims in the Nazi concentration camps. Anne Frank was denied a U.S. visa. Although this point has nothing to do with a serious historian's case for WWII as a Just War, it is so central to U.S. mythology that I'll include here a key passage from Nicholson Baker:

> "Anthony Eden, Britain's foreign secretary, who'd been tasked by Churchill with handling queries about refugees, dealt coldly with one of many important delegations, saying that any diplomatic effort to obtain the release of the Jews from Hitler was 'fantastically impossible.' On a trip to the United States, Eden candidly told Cordell Hull, the secretary of state, that the real difficulty with asking Hitler for the Jews was that 'Hitler might well take us up on any such offer, and there simply are not enough ships and means of transportation in the world to handle them.' Churchill

agreed. 'Even were we to obtain permission to withdraw all
the Jews,' he wrote in reply to one pleading letter, 'transport
alone presents a problem which will be difficult of solution.'
Not enough shipping and transport? Two years earlier, the
British had evacuated nearly 340,000 men from the beaches
of Dunkirk in just nine days. The U.S. Air Force had many
thousands of new planes. During even a brief armistice, the
Allies could have airlifted and transported refugees in very
large numbers out of the German sphere."[115]

Perhaps it does go to the question of "Right Intention" that the
"good" side of the war simply did not give a damn about what
would become the central example of the badness of the "bad" side
of the war.

4. The war was not defensive. FDR lied that he had a map of
Nazi plans to carve up South America, that he had a Nazi plan to
eliminate religion, that U.S. ships (covertly assisting British war
planes) were innocently attacked by Nazis, that Germany was a
threat to the United States.[116] A case can be made that the U.S.
needed to enter the war in Europe to defend other nations, which
had entered to defend yet other nations, but a case could also be
made that the U.S. escalated the targeting of civilians, extended
the war, and inflicted more damage than might have occurred,
had the U.S. done nothing, attempted diplomacy, or invested in
nonviolence. To claim that a Nazi empire could have grown to
someday include an occupation of the United States is wildly far
fetched and not borne out by any earlier or later examples from
other wars.

5. We now know much more widely and with much more data that nonviolent resistance to occupation and injustice is more likely to succeed—and that success more likely to last—than violent resistance. With this knowledge, we can look back at the stunning successes of nonviolent actions against the Nazis that were not well organized or built on beyond their initial successes.[117]

6. The Good War was not good for the troops. Lacking intense modern training and psychological conditioning to prepare soldiers to engage in the unnatural act of murder, some 80 percent of U.S. and other troops in World War II did not fire their weapons at "the enemy."[118] The fact that veterans of WWII were treated better after the war than other soldiers before or since, was the result of the pressure created by the Bonus Army after the previous war. That veterans were given free college, healthcare, and pensions was not due to the merits of the war or in some way a result of the war. Without the war, everyone could have been given free college for many years. If we provided free college to everyone today, it would then require much more than Hollywoodized World War II stories to get many people into military recruiting stations.

7. Several times the number of people killed in German camps were killed outside of them in the war. The majority of those people were civilians. The scale of the killing, wounding, and destroying made WWII the single worst thing humanity has ever done to itself in a short space of time. We imagine the allies were somehow "opposed" to the far lesser killing in the camps. But that can't justify the cure that was worse than the disease.

8. Escalating the war to include the all-out destruction of civilians and cities, culminating in the completely indefensible nuking of cities took WWII out of the realm of defensible projects for many who had defended its initiation—and rightly so. Demanding unconditional surrender and seeking to maximize death and suffering did immense damage and left a grim and foreboding legacy.

9. Killing huge numbers of people is supposedly defensible for the "good" side in a war, but not for the "bad" side. The distinction between the two is never as stark as fantasized. The United States had a long history as an apartheid state. U.S. traditions of oppressing African Americans, practicing genocide against Native Americans, and now interning Japanese Americans also gave rise to specific programs that inspired Germany's Nazis—these included camps for Native Americans, and programs of eugenics and human experimentation that existed before, during, and after the war. One of these programs included giving syphilis to people in Guatemala at the same time the Nuremberg trials were taking place.[119] The U.S. military hired hundreds of top Nazis at the end of the war; they fit right in.[120] The U.S. aimed for a wider world empire, before the war, during it, and ever since. German neo-Nazis today, forbidden to wave the Nazi flag, sometimes wave the flag of the Confederate States of America instead.

10. The "good" side of the "good war," the party that did most of the killing and dying for the winning side, was the communist Soviet Union. That doesn't make the war a triumph for communism, but it does tarnish Washington's and Hollywood's tales of triumph for "democracy."[121]

11. World War II still hasn't ended. Ordinary people in the United States didn't have their incomes taxed until World War II and that's never stopped. It was supposed to be temporary.[122] WWII-era bases built around the world have never closed. U.S. troops have never left Germany or Japan.[123] There are more than 100,000 U.S. and British bombs still in the ground in Germany, still killing.[124]

12. Going back 75 years to a nuclear-free, colonial world of completely different structures, laws, and habits to justify what has been the greatest expense of the United States in each of the years since is a bizarre feat of self-deception that isn't attempted in the justification of any lesser enterprise. Assume I've got numbers 1 through 11 totally wrong, and you've still got to explain how an event from the early 1940s justifies dumping a trillion 2017 dollars into war funding that could have been spent to feed, clothe, cure, and shelter millions of people, and to environmentally protect the earth.

THE U.S. REVOLUTION WAS NOT JUST

Many nations—including Canada as the nearest example—have gained their independence without wars. We claim that the "founding fathers" fought a war for independence, but if we could have had all the same advantages without the war, would that not have been better than killing tens of thousands of people?

Back in 1986, a book was published by the great nonviolent strategist Gene Sharp, now Virginia State Delegate David Toscano, and others, called *Resistance, Politics, and the American Struggle for Independence, 1765-1775.*

Those dates are not a typo. During those years, the people of the British colonies that would become the United States used boycotts, rallies, marches, theatrics, noncompliance, bans on imports and exports, parallel extra-legal governments, the lobbying of Parliament, the physical shutting down of courts and offices and ports, the destruction of tax stamps, endless educating and organizing, and the dumping of tea into a harbor—all to successfully achieve a large measure of independence, among other things, prior to the War for Independence. Home-spinning clothes to resist the British empire was practiced in the future United States long before Gandhi tried it.

The colonists didn't talk about their activities in Gandhian terms. They didn't foreswear violence. They sometimes threatened it and occasionally used it. They also, disturbingly, talked of resisting "slavery" to England even while maintaining actual slavery in the "New World." And they spoke of their loyalty to the King even while denouncing his laws.

Yet they largely rejected violence as counter-productive. They repealed the Stamp Act after effectively nullifying it. They repealed nearly all of the Townsend Acts. The committees they organized to enforce boycotts of British goods also enforced public safety and developed a new national unity. Prior to the battles of Lexington and Concord, the farmers of Western Massachusetts had nonviolently taken over all the court houses and booted the

British out. And then the Bostonians turned decisively to violence, a choice that need not be excused, much less glorified.

While we imagine that the Iraq War has been the only U.S. war started with lies, we forget that the Boston Massacre was distorted beyond recognition, including in an engraving by Paul Revere that depicted the British as butchers. We erase the fact that Benjamin Franklin produced a fake issue of the *Boston Independent* in which the British boasted of scalp hunting. And we forget the elite nature of the opposition to Britain. We drop down the memory hole the reality of those early days for ordinary nameless people. Howard Zinn explains:

> *"Around 1776, certain important people in the English colonies made a discovery that would prove enormously useful for the next two hundred years. They found that by creating a nation, a symbol, a legal unity called the United States, they could take over land, profits, and political power from favorites of the British Empire. In the process, they could hold back a number of potential rebellions and create a consensus of popular support for the rule of a new, privileged leadership."*[125]

In fact, prior to the violent revolution, there had been 18 uprisings against colonial governments, six black rebellions, and 40 riots. The political elites saw a possibility for redirecting anger toward England. The poor who would not profit from the war or reap its political rewards had to be compelled by force to fight in it. Many, including enslaved people, promised greater liberty by the British, deserted or switched sides.

Punishment for infractions in the Continental Army was 100 lashes. When George Washington, the richest man in America, was unable to convince Congress to raise the legal limit to 500 lashes, he considered using hard labor as a punishment instead, but dropped that idea because the hard labor would have been indistinguishable from regular service in the Continental Army. Soldiers also deserted because they needed food, clothing, shelter, medicine, and money. They signed up for pay, were not paid, and endangered their families' wellbeing by remaining in the Army unpaid. About two-thirds of them were ambivalent to or against the cause for which they were fighting and suffering. Popular rebellions, like Shays' Rebellion in Massachusetts, would follow the revolutionary victory.

The American revolutionaries were also able to open up the West to expansion and wars against the Native Americans, something the British had been forbidding. The American Revolution, the very act of birth and liberation for the United States, was also a war of expansion and conquest. King George, according to the Declaration of Independence, had "endeavoured (*sic*) to bring on the inhabitants of our frontiers, the merciless Indian Savages." Of course, those were people fighting in defense of their own lands and lives. Victory at Yorktown was bad news for the future of Native American nations.

The wars against Native Americans began immediately, as well as wars into Florida and Canada. The War of 1812 was intended to conquer the residents of Canada, who were expected to welcome U.S. invaders as liberators. Their actual response resembled that expectation even less than has the Iraqis' since 2003.

THE U.S. CIVIL WAR WAS NOT JUST

The U.S. Civil War was fought by the North—so many believe—in order to put an end to the evil of slavery. In reality, that goal was a belated excuse for a war already well underway, much like spreading democracy to Iraq became a belated justification for a war begun in 2003 overwhelmingly in the name of eliminating fictional weaponry. In fact, the mission of ending slavery was required to justify a war that had become too horrifying to be justified solely by the empty political goal of "union." Patriotism had not yet been puffed up into quite the enormity it is today. Casualties were mounting sharply: 25,000 at Shiloh, 20,000 at Bull Run, 24,000 in a day at Antietam. A week after Antietam, President Abraham Lincoln issued the Emancipation Proclamation, which freed the slaves only in the states that had seceded—where Lincoln could not free the slaves except by winning the war.

Yale historian Harry Stout explains why Lincoln took this step: "By Lincoln's calculation, the killing must continue on ever grander scales. But for that to succeed, the people must be persuaded to shed blood without reservation. This, in turn, required a moral certitude that the killing was just. Only emancipation—Lincoln's last card—would provide such certitude." The Proclamation also worked against Britain's entering the war on the side of the South.

Although ending slavery became the rationale or "cause" of continuing the war, the war did not, in fact, end slavery. As documented in Douglas Blackmon's book, *Slavery By Another Name: The Re-Enslavement of Black Americans from the Civil War to World War II*, the institution of slavery in the U.S. South largely ended for as long as 20 years in some places upon completion of the U.S. Civil War. And then it was back again, in a slightly different form, widespread, controlling, publicly known and accepted—right up to World War II. In fact, in other forms, it remains today. During widely publicized trials of slave owners for the crime of slavery in 1903—trials that did virtually nothing to end the pervasive practice—the *Montgomery Advertiser* editorialized: "Forgiveness is a Christian virtue and forgetfulness is often a relief, but some of us will never forgive nor forget the damnable and brutal excesses that were committed all over the South by negroes and their white allies, many of whom were federal officials, against whose acts our people were practically powerless."

This was a publicly acceptable position in Alabama in 1903: slavery should be tolerated because of the evils committed by the North during the war and during the occupation that followed. It's worth considering whether slavery might have been ended more quickly without a war. To say that is not, of course, to assert that in reality the pre-war United States was radically different than it was, that slave owners were willing to sell out, or that either side was open to a nonviolent solution. But most nations that ended slavery did so without a civil war. Some did it in the way that Washington, D.C. did it, through compensated emancipation.

Had the United States ended slavery without the war and without division, it would have avoided the bitter post-war resentment that has yet to die down. Ending racism would likely have been a very lengthy process, regardless. But that process might have been given a head start rather than an enormous hurdle. Our stubborn refusal to recognize the U.S. Civil War as a hindrance to freedom rather than the path to it, as a catastrophe that failed to end slavery but succeeded in creating lasting hatred, allows us to watch the U.S. military devastate places like Iraq and then to marvel at the duration of the resulting animosity.

Wars continue to claim new victims for many years after they end, even if all the cluster bombs are picked up. Had the Northern U.S. allowed the South to secede, ended the returning of "fugitive slaves," and used diplomatic and economic means to urge the South to abolish slavery, it seems reasonable to suppose that slavery might have lasted in the South beyond 1865, but very likely not until 1945 as occurred in reality. To say this is, once again, not to imagine that it actually happened, or that there weren't Northerners who opposed war for their own selfish reasons unrelated to the fate of enslaved African Americans. It is just to put into proper context the traditional defense of the Civil War as having murdered hundreds of thousands of people on both sides in order to accomplish the greater good of ending slavery.

After the Civil War, across most of the South, a system of petty, even meaningless, crimes, such as "vagrancy," created the threat of arrest for any black person. Upon arrest, a poor black man would be presented with an unpayable debt. His inability to pay meant being put into one of hundreds of forced labor camps. The alternative was to put oneself in debt to and under the protection of a white owner.

Slavery did not end. The 13th Amendment sanctions slavery for convicts, and no statute prohibited slavery—yes, actual slavery—until the 1950s. All that was needed for the pretense of legality was the equivalent of today's plea bargain.

Not only did slavery not end. For many thousands the conditions of the slavery were dramatically worsened. The antebellum slave owner typically had a financial interest in keeping an enslaved person alive and healthy enough to work. A mine or mill that purchased the work of hundreds of convicts had no interest in their futures beyond the term of their sentences. In fact, local governments would replace a convict who died with another, so there was no economic reason not to work them to death. Mortality rates for leased-out convicts in Alabama were as high as 45 percent per year. Some who died in mines were tossed into coke ovens rather than being buried at a cost to their employers.

Long after the "ending of slavery," enslaved Americans were bought and sold, chained by the ankles and necks at night, whipped to death, waterboarded, and murdered at the discretion of their owners, such as U.S. Steel Corporation which purchased mines near Birmingham where generations of "free" African Americans were worked to death underground.

Five days after the Japanese attack on Pearl Harbor, the U.S. government took legal actions to end slavery, to counter possible criticism from Germany or Japan. Five years after World War II, a group of former Nazis, some of whom had used slave labor in caves in Germany, were invited to set up shop in Alabama to work on creating new weapons technologies. They found the people of Alabama extremely forgiving of their past deeds.[126] This team of rocket scientists would later become the core of NASA (the National Aeronautics and Space Administration).[127]

To imagine slavery ending without war, we need only look at the actual history of various other countries. Slavery was ended more effectively without war—through compensated emancipation, for example—in the colonies of Britain, Denmark, France, and the Netherlands, and in most of South America and the Caribbean. That model also worked in Washington, D.C. Slave owning states in the United States rejected it, however, most of them choosing secession instead. That's the way history went, and many people would have had to think very differently for it to have gone otherwise. But the cost of freeing the slaves—by "buying" them and then granting their freedom—would have been far less than the North spent on the war. And that's not even counting what the South spent or factoring in human costs measured in deaths, injuries, mutilations, trauma, destruction, and decades of lasting bitterness.[128]

On June 20, 2013, the *Atlantic Magazine* published an article called "No, Lincoln Could Not Have 'Bought the Slaves.'"[129] Why not? Well, the slave owners didn't want to sell. That's perfectly true. They didn't, not at all. But *The Atlantic* focuses on another argument, namely that it would have just been too expensive, costing as much as $3 billion (in 1860s money). Yet, if you read closely—it's easy to miss it—the author admits that the war cost more than twice that amount. So, the cost of freeing everyone enslaved in the South was *not* unaffordable, especially when compared to the cost of the Civil

War. If—radically contrary to actual history—U.S. slave owners had opted to end slavery without war, it's hard to imagine that as a bad decision for any of the parties involved.

The point is not so much that our ancestors could have made a different choice (they were nowhere near doing so), but that their choice looks foolish from our point of view. If tomorrow we were to wake up and discover a large majority of the populace appropriately outraged over the horror of mass incarceration, would it help to find some large fields in which to kill each other off in large numbers to abolish prisons? What would that have to do with abolishing prisons? And what did the Civil War have to do with abolishing slavery?

Let me try to really, really emphasize this point: compensated emancipation did not happen and was not about to happen, was nowhere remotely close to happening; but its happening would have been a good thing. Had slave owners and politicians radically altered their thinking and chosen to end slavery without a war, they would have ended it with less suffering, and probably ended it more completely. Try to imagine big changes being made in our society today, whether it's closing prisons, creating solar arrays, rewriting the Constitution, facilitating sustainable agriculture, publicly financing elections, or developing democratic media outlets (you may not like any of these ideas, but I'm sure you can think of a major change that you would like). Can you imagine a path to these goals that would begin with Step 1 "Find large fields in which to make our children kill each other"? Instead, why not skip right by that to Step 2 "Do the thing that needs doing"?

We can't know for certain what would have happened to the colonies without the revolution or to slavery without the Civil War. But we know that much of the rest of the hemisphere ended colonial rule and slavery without wars. Had Congress found the decency to end slavery through legislation alone (it did pass the relevant legislation after fighting a pointless war), perhaps the nation would have ended slavery without division. Had the U.S. South been permitted to secede in peace, and the Fugitive Slave Law been easily repealed by the North, it seems unlikely slavery would have lasted much longer. The pressures of international morality and of industrialization were against it. What brought the matter to a crisis in the United States was not just a disagreement over slavery, but an agreement on imperialism. Had the North and South been content with the existing size of the country, there would have been no war, at least not in 1860. The conflict was, at that point, over the question of expanding slavery into new territories. That conflict had been fueled by a previous war that had stolen half of Mexico for the purpose of expanding slavery.

WAR ON YUGOSLAVIA WAS NOT JUST

As quoted above, Allman and Winright cite Kosovo, on the moral authority of the United Nations, as a "humanitarian" war, the one Just War that has actually happened in recent history. But according to Michael Mandel, author of *How America Gets Away With Murder: Illegal Wars, Collateral Damage, and Crimes Against Humanity,* "The notion of a 'humanitarian war' would have rung in the ears of the drafters of the UN Charter as nothing short of

Hitlerian, because it was precisely the justification used by Hitler himself for the invasion of Poland just six years earlier."

A few inconvenient truths: The United Nations did not authorize the United States and its NATO allies to bomb Serbia, in the former Yugoslavia, in 1999. Neither did the United States Congress. And, just as I was drafting this book in August 2016, the former president of Serbia Slobodan Milosevic—arch-villain of the Western media, called a "new Hitler" by Tony Blair—was, in a manner, posthumously exonerated, within a lengthy ruling on another defendant, by the UN-established International Criminal Tribunal for the Former Yugoslavia. (This exoneration does not, of course, alter Milosevic's having been in many other ways a horrible ruler.)[130]

While many ordinary people in the United States and Europe supported or tolerated the 1999 Kosovo bombing out of good intentions—that is, because they believed the propaganda—the motivations and actions of the U.S. government and NATO turn out to have been as cynical and immoral as usual.

The United States worked vigorously for the breakup of Yugoslavia and intentionally prevented negotiated agreements among the parties. The U.S. engaged in a massive bombing campaign that killed large numbers of people, injured many more, destroyed civilian infrastructure, hospitals, and media outlets, and created a refugee crisis. This destruction was accomplished through lies, fabrications, and exaggerations about atrocities, and then justified anachronistically as a response to violence that it generated.

After the bombing, the U.S. allowed the Bosnian Muslims to agree to a peace plan very similar to the plan that the U.S. had been blocking prior to the bombing spree. Here's U.N. Secretary General Boutros Boutros-Ghali:

> *"In its first weeks in office, the Clinton administration had administered a death blow to the Vance-Owen plan that would have given the Serbs 43 percent of the territory of a unified state. In 1995 at Dayton, the administration took pride in an agreement that, after nearly three more years of horror and slaughter, gave the Serbs 49 percent in a state partitioned into two entities."*[131]

Not exactly a ringing endorsement.

We were told that NATO had to bomb Yugoslavia to prevent a genocide. But then why sabotage negotiations? Why pull out all the U.N. observers? Why bomb away from the area of the supposed genocide? Why give five days' warning? Wouldn't a real rescue operation, even a militarized one, have sent in ground forces without any warning, while continuing diplomatic efforts? Wouldn't a humanitarian effort have avoided killing so many men, women, and children with bombs, while threatening to starve whole populations through sanctions?

My former Congressman Tom Perriello sees the 1999 Kosovo war as a good example of evading the requirements of the United Nations—not to mention Congressional opposition and the U.S. Constitution—for the good of humanity:

"In many ways, the 1999 Kosovo War represents the meeting place of nimble force and modern multilateral engagement. . . . The air campaign included targeting of key installations— military and infrastructure—that crippled the Serbs' efforts to complete the ethnic cleansing of Kosovo Albanians. The campaign was stunningly successful in stopping the atrocities on the ground through air power, producing no U.S. casualties and civilian casualty estimates ranging from 20 to 500 deaths. Not just the volume but the ratio changed— civilian casualties have generally, and often dramatically, outnumbered combatant casualties in modern warfare, but that flipped decisively in the case of Kosovo. While the war left in its wake reprisal killings and hundreds of thousands of displaced people, most humanitarian experts have acknowledged that it was a solid example of rapid, decisive, multilateral action to stop widespread and systematic crimes against humanity."

Let's back up and give this a little context. When, in 1995, Croatia had slaughtered or "ethnically cleansed" Serbs with Washington's blessing, driving 150,000 people from their homes, we weren't supposed to notice, much less drop bombs to prevent it. The bombing was saved for Milosevic, who—we were falsely told in 1999—refused to negotiate peace and therefore had to be bombed. We were not told that the United States was insisting on an agreement that no nation in the world would voluntarily agree to, one giving NATO complete freedom to occupy all of Yugoslavia with absolute immunity from laws for all of its personnel. In the June 14, 1999 issue of *The Nation*, George Kenney, a former State Department Yugoslavia desk officer, reported: "An unimpeachable press source who regularly travels with Secretary of State Madeleine Albright told this [writer] that, swearing reporters to deep-background confidentiality at the Rambouillet talks, a senior State Department official had bragged that the United States 'deliberately set the bar higher than the Serbs could accept.' The Serbs needed, according to the official, a little bombing to see reason." Jim Jatras, a foreign policy aide to Senate Republicans, reported in a May 18, 1999, speech at the Cato Institute in Washington that he had it "on good authority" that a "senior Administration official told media at Rambouillet, under embargo" the following: "We intentionally set the bar too high for the Serbs to comply. They need some bombing, and that's what they are going to get." In interviews with FAIR (Fairness and Accuracy in Reporting), both Kenney and Jatras asserted that these were actual quotes transcribed by reporters who spoke with a U.S. official.[132]

What happens when the search for opportunities for humanitarian wars leads us to avoid opportunities for humanitarian peace? In the case of the 1999 bombing, what happened was a solution to small-scale killing that constituted and predictably led to large-scale killing and the creation of refugees. While the sequence of events is often inverted in the telling, this was a humanitarian catastrophe in the guise of a humanitarian rescue.[133]

In the year prior to the bombing some 2,000 people were killed, a majority by Kosovo Liberation Army guerrillas who, with support from the CIA, were seeking to incite a Serbian response that would appeal to Western humanitarian warriors. At the same time, NATO member Turkey was committing much larger atrocities, with 80% of their weapons coming from the United States. But Washington didn't want war with Turkey, so no propaganda campaign was built around its crimes; instead weapons shipments to Turkey were increased.

In contrast, a slick propaganda campaign regarding Kosovo established a model that would be followed in future wars, by connecting exaggerated and fictional atrocities to the Nazi holocaust. A photo of a thin man seen through barbed wire was reproduced endlessly. But investigative journalist Philip Knightly determined that it was probably the reporters and photographers who were behind the barbed wire, and that the place photographed, while ugly, was a refugee camp that people, including the fat man standing next to the thin man, were free to leave. There were indeed atrocities, but most of them occurred after the bombing, not before it. Most of Western reporting inverted that chronology.

WAR ON LIBYA IS NOT JUST

White House lawyer Harold Koh told Congress that an aerial attack on Libya would not be a real war or even "hostilities" because U.S. troops would not be on the ground. He had just invented that definition of wars and hostilities. U.S. troops were already on the ground in Libya stirring up trouble.[134]

MSNBC's Ed Schultz demanded war against the evil of formerly U.S.-backed dictator Muammar Gaddafi. Juan Cole and Chris Hedges favored the same war for humanitarian reasons (though Hedges turned around and opposed it later, writing an excellent article against it six months in).[135]

The White House claimed that Gaddafi had threated to massacre the people of Benghazi with "no mercy," but the *New York Times* and other news outlets reported that Gaddafi's threat was directed at rebel fighters, not civilians, and that Gaddafi promised amnesty for those "who throw their weapons away."[136] Gaddafi also offered to allow rebel fighters to escape to Egypt if they preferred not to fight to the death. Yet President Obama warned of imminent genocide.

The above report of what Gaddafi really threatened fits with his past behavior. There were other opportunities for massacres had he wished to commit massacres—in Zawiya, Misurata, and Ajdabiya. He did not do so. After extensive fighting in Misurata, a report by Human Rights Watch made clear that Gaddafi had targeted fighters, not civilians. Of 400,000 people in Misurata, 257 died in two months of fighting. Out of 949 wounded, less than 3 percent were women.

It wasn't genocide that was looming. It was the imminent defeat of the rebels, the same anti-Gaddafi rebels who warned Western media of the looming genocide, the same rebels who the *New York Times* said "feel no loyalty to the truth in shaping their propaganda" and who were "making vastly inflated claims of [Gaddafi's] barbaric behavior." The result of NATO joining the war was probably more killing, not less. It certainly extended a war that looked likely to end soon with a victory for Gaddafi.

Alan Kuperman pointed out in the *Boston Globe* that "Obama embraced the noble principle of the responsibility to protect—

which some quickly dubbed the Obama Doctrine—calling for intervention when possible to prevent genocide. Libya reveals how this approach, implemented reflexively, may backfire by encouraging rebels to provoke and exaggerate atrocities, to entice intervention that ultimately perpetuates civil war and humanitarian suffering."[137]

As noted above, in March 2011, the African Union had a plan for peace in Libya but was prevented by NATO from traveling to Libya to discuss it until April. After Gaddafi had been sodomized with a knife and murdered, and the country thrown into chaos, with weapons proliferating around the region, U.S. Secretary of State Hillary Clinton proclaimed "We came. We saw. He died!" laughing triumphantly. Her emails, later leaked, showed her concern in Libya to be more about oil than human rights.[138] They also showed that overthrow had been the goal from the start, with Clinton adviser Sidney Blumenthal going so far as to recommend "shock and awe." Blumenthal recommended that Clinton drop any more talk of the supposed rescue of people in Benghazi. He proposed no new humanitarian arguments, only geopolitical, balance-of-power stuff. He also pointed out that the overthrow could likely result in a "jihadist resurgence" and growth for al Qaeda. And he expressed awareness of summary executions by the rebels the U.S. was backing, but neither he nor Clinton expressed any concern about those atrocities.

The U.S. public, to its credit and without needing to see Clinton's emails, opposed the war (in polls), as did Congress and the United Nations (in the sense of not authorizing it) while doing nothing to stop it. The U.N. authorized a fraudulent "rescue mission," not the overthrow that immediately and predictably followed. Libya was predictably reduced to violence and chaos, which gave rise to a refugee crisis.[139] The United States, as I write, is trying to fix the current disaster in Libya with the same tool that created it: more bombing.

Former Congressman Perriello holds up the disastrous and illegal bombing of Libya as a Just War: "The fledgling legitimacy innovations of the Kosovo campaign proved to be fully grown by the time Moammar Gaddafi moved to brutally crush popular uprisings. . . . In a rare convergence of international condemnation and an even rarer willingness to back that up with action, the Arab League, NATO, and UN Security Council demanded that Gaddafi relinquish power to prevent the slaughter of civilians." The U.N. Security Council demanded nothing of the sort. It demanded a no-fly zone and an arms embargo, not the overthrow of Gaddafi, much less his murder. The supposed prevention of an atrocity was used to create a U.N. resolution that did not include overthrowing the government, but that resolution was used to overthrow the government.

Don't let facts stand in Perriello's way: "Today, Gaddafi is dead, and the Libyan people have their first chance for democratic, accountable governance in decades." Any time you overthrow a dictator, including one that the United States had been arming and supporting like Gaddafi, you can declare a "chance" at democracy. But when the overthrow has been violent and accomplished by backing groups with little interest in democracy, the chance is

Psalm 144:1
Blessed be the Lord
my Rock, who trains
my hands for war,
my fingers for battle

very slim. Even setting aside the tool you've provided for people like Perriello to prop up a trillion-dollar U.S. military complex, even setting aside the destruction of international law that Perriello celebrates, and even setting aside the chaos and killing yet to come, what is it that you've accomplished? You've turned a relatively minor but much exaggerated crisis that your long-standing policies helped to create, into an excuse to bomb a nation and overthrow its government. But why set all the larger results aside? You've diverted resources from nonviolent activism, actual humanitarian aid, and diplomacy to force as if force were all there is. Perriello tells us so:

> *"Progressives often demand action in the face of abject human suffering, but we know from recent history that in some situations moral condemnation, economic sanctions, or ex-post tribunals don't save lives. Only force does."*

Only force saves lives. Apartheid should not have been allowed to end in South Africa without a civil war. India should never have been permitted to throw out Britain without more bloodshed. The

U.S. Civil Rights movement should have used rocket launchers. The Arab Spring in Tunisia should be undone and re-begun with snipers and tanks. Perriello doesn't say these things, but they are implied by the framework in which one must often choose between war or nothing.

WAR ON RWANDA WOULD NOT HAVE BEEN JUST

Allman and Winright, and Perriello, cite Rwanda as a war that would have been just. Writes Perriello: "During this same period, we have been reminded tragically of the real and staggering human cost of inaction, most notably in the 800,000 lives lost in Rwanda. The tendency to feel less moral responsibility for the results of inaction and to overvalue the risks of acting in difficult situations is natural, but it is ultimately indefensible."

Very true. But his analysis requires ignoring the many actions the United States did take. The fact is that the United States cannot really "intervene" anywhere, because it has already long since been there creating the supposed need for intervention. I recommend a book by Robin Philpot called *Rwanda and the New Scramble for Africa: From Tragedy to Useful Imperial Fiction*. Philpot opens with U.N. Secretary General Boutros Boutros-Ghali's comment that "the genocide in Rwanda was one hundred percent the responsibility of the Americans!"

How could that be? Americans are not to blame for how things are in backward parts of the world prior to their "interventions."

Surely Mr. double Boutros has got his chronology wrong. Too much time spent in those U.N. offices with foreign anti-American bureaucrats no doubt. And yet, the facts—not disputed claims but universally agreed upon facts that are simply deemphasized by many—say otherwise.

The United States quietly backed an invasion of Rwanda on October 1, 1990, by a Ugandan army led by U.S.-trained killers, and supported their attack on Rwanda for three-and-a-half years. Have Allman and Winright or Perriello ever disputed that? I don't think they've even mentioned it.

The Rwandan government, in response, did not follow the model of the U.S. internment of Japanese during World War II, or of U.S. treatment of Muslims for the past 15 years. Nor did it fabricate the idea of traitors in its midst (the invading army in fact had 36 active cells of collaborators in Rwanda). But the Rwandan government did arrest 8,000 people and hold them for a few days to six-months. Africa Watch (later Human Rights Watch/Africa) declared this a serious violation of human rights, but had nothing to say about the invasion and war. Alison Des Forges of Africa Watch explained that good human rights groups "do not examine the issue of who makes war. We see war as an evil and we try to prevent the existence of war from being an excuse for massive human rights violations." (See my explanation of the harm done by the *ad bellum* / *in bello* distinction above.)

The war killed many people, whether or not those killings qualified as human rights violations. People fled the invaders, creating a huge refugee crisis, ruined agriculture, a wrecked economy, and a shattered society. The United States and the West armed the war makers and applied additional pressure through the World Bank, IMF, and USAID. And among the results of the war was increased hostility between Hutus and Tutsis. Eventually the government would topple. First would come the mass slaughter known as the Rwandan Genocide. And before that would come the murder of two presidents. At that point, in April 1994, Rwanda was in chaos almost on the level of "post-liberation" Iraq or Libya.

One way to have prevented the slaughter would have been to not support the war. Another way to have prevented the slaughter would have been to not support the assassination of the presidents of Rwanda and Burundi on April 6, 1994. The evidence points strongly to the U.S.-backed and U.S.-trained war-maker Paul Kagame—now president of Rwanda—as the guilty party. While there is no dispute that the presidents' plane was shot down, human rights groups and international bodies have simply referred in passing to a "plane crash" and refused to investigate.

A third way to have prevented the slaughter, which began immediately upon news of the presidents' assassinations, might have been to send in nonpartisan, nonviolent peaceworkers or even U.N. peacekeepers (not the same thing, be it noted, as the Hellfire missiles for which the myth of "Rwanda" has been so frequently invoked), but that was not what Washington wanted, and the U.S. government worked against it. What the Clinton administration was after was putting Kagame in power. Thus the resistance to calling the slaughter a "genocide" (and sending in the U.N.) until blaming that crime on the Hutu-dominated government was deemed useful.

The evidence assembled by Philpot suggests that the "genocide," while perfectly real and horrific, was not so much planned as something that erupted after the presidential plane was shot down. It was politically motivated rather than simply ethnic, and was not nearly as one-sided as generally assumed. Moreover, the killing of civilians in Rwanda has continued ever since, although the killing has been much heavier in neighboring Congo, where Kagame's government took the war—with U.S. aid and weapons and troops—and bombed refugee camps killing roughly a million people. The excuse for going into the Congo has been the hunt for Rwandan war criminals. The real motivation has been Western control and profits from the country's resources.[140] War in the Congo has continued to this day, leaving some 6 million dead— the worst killing since the estimated 70 million of WWII. And yet almost nobody ever says "We must prevent another Congo!"

WAR ON SUDAN WOULD NOT HAVE BEEN JUST

Allman and Winright raise the question of whether a military overthrow should have been (or still should be?) used in Sudan in response to the crisis of violence and suffering of recent years.[141]

The useful thing this sort of idea does is expose hypocrisy on the part of Western governments. Their choice to bomb certain countries, worsening the populace's suffering, is based on economic and military interests, not on the extent of the humanitarian need. A Just War theorist is right to suggest that perhaps there is as much suffering in Sudan as in Yemen, so that perhaps Sudan is worthy of being bombed too.

But that doesn't mean that bombing or a ground war or any kind of war would actually help. Where did the weapons come from? When and how would escalated violence end? Why would Sudan be the first place in which one of these wars improves things? What makes it different from all the other countries the Pentagon has proposed to "help"?

Why is it always a war that didn't happen that we're told to imagine succeeding? Why do we hear so little about Haiti as a model for Just War? Or Korea? Or Panama? Or Afghanistan? How is rescuing people from ISIS by bombing them working out?

WAR ON ISIS IS NOT JUST

"Another [opportunity for a Just War] would be the threat posed by ISIS to Christians and others in Iraq and Syria, extreme situations from which perpetrators and victims alike need to be rescued." So write Mark Allman and Tobias Winright. Why Christians? Are we expected to care more about Christians? And why ISIS as opposed to, say, Saudi Arabia? Why pick ISIS out of all the extreme situations in which rulers are brutally murdering and torturing?

Two years ago, blogger John Horgan asked me for a paragraph on what to do about ISIS. I sent him this fairly long one:

I'd say start by recognizing where ISIS came from. The U.S. and its junior partners destroyed Iraq, left a sectarian division, poverty, desperation, and an illegitimate government in Baghdad that did not represent Sunnis or other groups. Then the U.S. armed and trained ISIS and allied groups in Syria, while continuing to prop up the Baghdad government, providing Hellfire missiles with which to attack Iraqis in Fallujah and elsewhere. ISIS has religious adherents but also opportunistic supporters who see it as the force resisting an unwanted rule from Baghdad and who increasingly see it as resisting the United States. It is in possession of U.S. weaponry provided directly to it in Syria and seized from the Iraqi government. At last count by the U.S. government, 79% of weapons transferred to Middle Eastern governments come from the United States, not counting transfers to groups like ISIS, and not counting weapons in the possession of the United States. So, the first thing to do differently going forward: stop bombing nations into ruins, and stop shipping weapons into the area you've left in chaos. Libya is of course another example of the disasters that U.S. wars leave behind them—a war, by the way, with U.S. weapons used on both sides, and a war launched on the pretext of a claim well documented to have been false that Gaddafi was threatening to massacre civilians. So, here's the next thing to do: be very skeptical of humanitarian claims. The U.S. bombing around Erbil to protect Kurdish and U.S. oil interests was initially justified as bombing to protect people on a mountain. But most of those people on the mountain were in no need of rescue, and that justification was quickly set aside, just as Benghazi was, in order to move on to wider war making for other purposes. Recall also that Obama was forced to withdraw U.S. troops from Iraq when he couldn't get the Iraqi government to give them immunity for crimes they commit. He has now obtained that immunity and back in they go, the crimes preceding them in the form of 500-pound bombs. While trying to rescue hostages and discovering an empty house, and racing to a mountain to save 30,000 people but finding 3,000 and most of those not wanting to leave, the U.S. claims to know exactly whom the 500-pound bombs are killing. But whoever they are killing, they are generating more enemies, and they are building support for ISIS, not diminishing it. So, now the U.S. finds itself on the opposite side of the war in Syria, so what does it do? Flip sides! Now the great moral imperative is not to bomb Assad but to bomb in defense of Assad, the only consistent point being that "something must be done" and the only conceivable something is to pick some party and bomb it. But why is that the only conceivable thing to be done? I can think of some others:

1. *Apologize for brutalizing the leader of ISIS in Abu Ghraib and to every other prisoner victimized under U.S. occupation*

2. *Apologize for destroying the nation of Iraq and to every family there*

3. *Begin making restitution by delivering aid (not "military aid" but actual aid, food, medicine) to the entire nation of Iraq*

4. *Apologize for the U.S. role in destabilizing Syria*

5. *Begin making restitution by delivering actual aid to Syria*

6. *Announce a commitment not to provide weapons to Iraq or Syria or Israel or Jordan or Egypt or Bahrain or any other nation anywhere on earth and to begin withdrawing U.S. troops from foreign territories and seas, including Afghanistan. (The U.S. Coast Guard in the Persian Gulf has clearly forgotten where the coast of the U.S. is!)*

7. Announce a commitment to invest heavily in solar, wind, and other green energy and to provide the same to democratic representative governments.

8. Begin providing Iran with free wind and solar technologies—at much lower cost of course than what it is costing the U.S. and Israel to threaten Iran over a nonexistent nuclear weapons program.

9. End economic sanctions that impact the people of Syria, Iran, Russia, and other nations.

10. Send diplomats to Baghdad and Damascus to negotiate aid and to encourage serious reforms.

11. Send journalists, aid workers, peaceworkers, human shields, and negotiators into crisis zones, understanding that this means risking lives, but that further militarization would risk a greater number of lives.

12. Empower people with agricultural assistance, education, cameras, and internet access.

13. Launch a communications campaign in the United States to replace military recruitment campaigns, focused on building sympathy and desire to serve as critical aid workers, persuading doctors and engineers to volunteer their time to travel to crisis areas.

14. Work through the United Nations on all of this.

15. Sign the United States on to the International Criminal Court and voluntarily propose the prosecution of top U.S. officials of this and the preceding regimes for their crimes.

OUR ANCESTORS LIVED IN A DIFFERENT CULTURAL WORLD

How should we think about the people who made wars in the past? I'd say similarly to how we think about people who engaged in environmental destruction or slavery or discrimination against women or dueling or blood feuds or trial by ordeal or lynching or human sacrifice or corporal punishment or now-dead religions or cruelty to animals. Some slave owners were more cruel than others. Some had deeper hypocritical regrets. But all were engaged in something we have tried to outgrow. Some war makers did a better job than others of attaching their wars to just causes, even if those causes might have been better advanced by other means. But all war makers were engaged in something we must try to outgrow. We can scorn their barbarism or forgive their ignorance, while—one hopes—recognizing that future scholars may do the same to us. But move on we must. And part of how we may be able to move on is by recognizing that we now have widespread awareness of alternatives to war, something that many who went before us did not.[142]

WE CAN AGREE ON JUST PEACE MAKING

"An unjust peace is better than a just war."
—*Marcus Tullius Cicero*

Yes an unjust peace is better than any war. But a just peace is even better. And here's where I agree wholeheartedly with Mark Allman and Tobias Winright, and where I propose that we all join

in collectively redirecting our energy. Just Peace Making should be our academic and practical obsession, not Just War. Allman and Winright themselves propose that the "pacifists and just war theorists" join together on this, which I eagerly agree to do (even if they call me a pacifist :-).

What if, instead of building up troops, weapons, and alliances to encircle Russia and China, the U.S. government were seeking paths to avoid future wars? If a war develops with Russia in the future, how many of us will be able to say we opposed the expansion of NATO, that we condemned and resisted the installation of missile bases in Romania and Poland, that we denounced the coup in Ukraine and stood in solidarity with those resisting violence and division there, that we sought to expose NATO's aggression and the military exercises near the border of Russia? At the same time, we must oppose Russia's militarized responses and its murderous war making, just like that of the United States, in Syria.

Allman and Winright propose working on forgiveness, public acknowledgment, apologies, punishment of war crimes (or as I would put it, the crime of war), amnesty, reconciliation, compensation, and environmental cleanup. I couldn't agree more. This portion of their book is no fun for me to argue with because I think it's exactly right and recommend reading it. I will add here, however, in a spirit of agreement, a talk I gave in a catholic church in Minnesota this summer:

An atheist's sermon on Luke 7:36-50 delivered at Saint Joan of Arc in Minneapolis, Minn., on June 12, 2016.

Forgiveness is a universal need, among those of us who are not religious and among believers in every religion on Earth. We must forgive each other our differences, and we must forgive much more difficult occurrences.

Some things we can forgive easily—by which, of course, I mean eliminating resentment from our hearts, not granting an eternal reward. If someone kissed my feet and poured oil on them and begged me to forgive her, frankly, I would have a harder time forgiving the kisses and oil than forgiving her a life of prostitution—which is, after all, not an act of cruelty toward me but the violation of a taboo into which she was likely compelled by hardship.

But to forgive men who were torturing and killing me on a cross? That I would be very unlikely to succeed at, especially as my nearing end—in the absence of a crowd to influence—might convince me of the pointlessness of making my last thought a magnanimous one. As long as I live, however, I intend to work on forgiveness.

If our culture truly developed the habit of forgiveness, it would dramatically improve our personal lives. It would also make wars impossible, which would further dramatically improve our personal lives. I think we have to forgive both those who we think have wronged us personally, and those whom our government has told us to hate, both at home and abroad.

I suspect I could find well over 100 million Christians in the United States who do not hate the men who crucified Jesus, but who do hate and would be highly offended at the idea of forgiving Adolf Hitler.

When John Kerry says that Bashar al Assad is Hitler, does that help you feel forgiving toward Assad? When Hillary Clinton says that Vladimir Putin is Hitler, does that help you relate to Putin as a human being? When ISIS cuts a man's throat with a knife, does your culture expect of you forgiveness or vengeance?

Forgiveness is not the only approach one can take to curing war fever, and not the one I usually try. Usually the case that's made for a war involves specific lies that can be exposed, such as lies about who used chemical weapons in Syria or who shot down an airplane in Ukraine.

Usually there is a great deal of hypocrisy one can point to. Was Assad already Hitler when he was torturing people for the CIA, or did he become Hitler by defying the U.S. government? Was Putin already Hitler before he refused to join in the 2003 attack on Iraq? If a particular ruler who has fallen out of favor is Hitler, what about all the brutal dictators whom the United States is arming and supporting? Are they all Hitler too?

Usually there is aggression by the United States that can be pointed to. The U.S. has aimed to overthrow the Syrian government for years and avoided negotiations for the nonviolent removal of Assad in favor of a violent overthrow believed to be imminent year after year. The U.S. has pulled out of arms reduction treaties with Russia, expanded NATO to its border, facilitated a coup in Ukraine, launched war games along the Russian border, put ships in the Black and Baltic Seas, moved more nukes into Europe, begun talking about smaller, more "usable" nukes, and set up missile bases in Romania and (under construction) in Poland. Imagine if Russia had done these things in North America.

Usually one can point out that no matter how evil a foreign ruler is, a war will kill large numbers of people unfortunate enough to be ruled by him—people who are innocent of his crimes.

But what if we tried the approach of forgiveness? Can one forgive ISIS its horrors? And would doing so result in free rein for more such horrors, or in their reduction or elimination?

The first question is easy. Yes, you can forgive ISIS its horrors. At least some people can. I feel no hatred toward ISIS. There are people who lost loved ones on 9/11 who quickly began advocating against any vengeful war. There are people who've lost loved ones to small-scale murder and opposed cruel punishment of the guilty party, even coming to know and care for the murderer. There are cultures that treat injustice as something in need of reconciliation rather than retribution.

Of course, the fact that others can do it doesn't mean that you can or should do it. But it's worth recognizing how right were those family members of 9/11 victims who opposed war. Now several hundred times as many people have been killed, and the hatred toward the United States that contributed to 9/11 has been multiplied accordingly. A global war on terrorism has predictably and indisputably increased terrorism.

If we take a deep breath and think seriously, we can also recognize that the resentment that calls out for forgiveness is not rational. Toddlers with guns kill more people in the United States than do foreign terrorists. But we don't hate toddlers. We don't bomb toddlers and whoever's near them. We don't think of toddlers as inherently evil or backward or belonging to the wrong religion. We forgive them instantly, without struggle. It's not their fault the guns were left lying around.

But is it the fault of ISIS that Iraq was destroyed? That Libya was thrown into chaos? That the region was flooded with U.S.-made weapons? That future ISIS leaders were tortured in U.S. camps?

That life was made into a nightmare? Maybe not, but it was their fault they murdered people. They are adults. They know what they are doing.

Do they? Remember, Jesus said they did not. He said, "Forgive them for they know not what they do." How could they possibly know what they are doing when they do things as truly awful as what they have done?

When U.S. officials retire and quickly blurt out that U.S. efforts are creating more enemies than they are killing, it becomes clear that attacking ISIS is counterproductive. It also becomes clear that at least some people engaged in it know that. But they also know what advances their careers, what provides for their families, what pleases their associates, and what benefits a certain sector of the U.S. economy. And they can always hold out hope that perhaps the next war will be the one that finally works. Do they really know what they do? How could they?

When President Obama sent a missile from a drone to blow up an American boy from Colorado named Abdulrahman al Awlaki, one should not imagine that his head or the heads of those seated too close to him remained on their bodies. That this boy wasn't killed with a knife shouldn't make his killing any more or less forgivable. We should desire no revenge against Barack Obama or John Brennan. But we should not limit our outraged demand for truth, restorative justice, and the replacement of murderous with peaceful public policies.

A U.S. Air Force officer recently said that a tool that would allow dropping food accurately to starving people in Syria would not be *used for such a purely humanitarian operation because it costs $60,000.[143] Yet the U.S. military is blowing through tens of billions of dollars on killing people there, and hundreds of billions of dollars every year on maintaining the ability to do the same all over the world. We've got CIA-trained troops in Syria fighting Pentagon-trained troops in Syria, and—as a matter of principle—we can't spend money on preventing starvation.*

Imagine living in Iraq or Syria and reading that. Imagine reading the comments of Congress members who support militarism because it supposedly provides jobs. Imagine living under a constantly buzzing drone in Yemen, no longer allowing your children to go to school or to go outside the house at all.

Now imagine forgiving the United States government. Imagine bringing yourself to see what looks like massive evil as in fact bureaucratic mishaps, systemic momentum, partisan blindness, and manufactured unawareness. Could you, as an Iraqi, forgive? I've seen Iraqis do it.

We in the United States can forgive the Pentagon. Can we forgive ISIS? And if not, why not? Can we forgive Saudis who look and sound like, and who support, ISIS, but who our televisions tell us are good loyal allies? If so, is it because we haven't seen Saudi victims of beheading or because of what those victims look like? If not, is it because of what Saudis look like?

If forgiveness came naturally to us, if we could do it immediately for ISIS, and therefore instantly for the neighbor who makes too much noise or votes for the wrong candidate, then marketing campaigns for wars would not work. Neither would campaigns to pack more Americans into prisons.

Forgiveness would not eliminate conflict, but it would render conflicts civil and nonviolent—exactly what the peace movement of the 1920s had in mind when it moved Frank Kellogg of St. Paul, Minnesota, to create the treaty that bans all war.

We need peace in ourselves and in our families. But we need to be wary of the attitude taken by a school board member in Virginia who said he'd support a celebration of peace as long as everyone understood he wasn't opposing any wars. We need reminders that peace begins with the abolition of war. I hope you'll join us.

HERE ARE SOME BOOKS WORTH READING

Beyond War: The Human Potential for Peace by Douglas Fry (2009)

Living Beyond War by Winslow Myers (2009)

War Is A Lie by David Swanson (2010)

The End of War by John Horgan (2012)

Transition to Peace by Russell Faure-Brac (2012)

War No More: The Case for Abolition by David Swanson (2013)

Shift: The Beginning of War, the Ending of War by Judith Hand (2013)

War and Delusion: A Critical Examination by Lauri Calhoun (2013)

War: A Crime Against Humanity by Roberto Vivo (2014)

Catholic Realism and the Abolition of War by David Carroll Cochran (2014)

A Global Security System: An Alternative to War by World Beyond War (2015)

War Is A Lie: Second Edition by David Swanson (April 5, 2016)

ACKNOWLDGEMENTS

My thanks for reading all or part of a draft of this and sending me comments and resources goes to Rose Marie Berger, Leah Bolger, Jeff Cohen, Marie Dennis, Pat Elder, Ted Grimsrud, Patrick Hiller, Raed Jarrar, Kathy Kelly, Eli McCarthy, Jim Rauner, Gar Smith, and Linda Swanson. All shortcomings are, of course, my own.

ABOUT THE AUTHOR

David Swanson is an author, activist, journalist, and radio host. He is director of WorldBeyondWar.org and campaign coordinator for RootsAction.org. Swanson's books include *War Is A Lie* and *When the World Outlawed War*. He blogs at DavidSwanson.org and WarIsACrime.org. He hosts Talk Nation Radio. He is a 2015 and 2016 Nobel Peace Prize Nominee.

ENDNOTES

1 Reports and photos from the Rome meeting:
https://nonviolencejustpeace.net
2 Ken Sehested, *Prayer and Politiks,* "Public reasoning and ekklesial reckoning: Commentary on the Vatican conference calling for 'spirituality and practice of active nonviolence' to displace church focus on just war," May 12, 2016, http://www.prayerandpolitiks. org/articles-essays-sermons/2016/05/12/public-reasoning-and-ekklesial-reckoning.2006877
3 Mark J. Allman & Tobias L. Winright, *After the Smoke Clears: The Just War Tradition and Post War Justice* (Maryknoll, N.Y.: Orbis Books, 2010) p. 138.
4 Mark J. Allman and Tobias Winright, "Protect Thy Neighbor," Commonweal Magazine, June 2, 2016, https://www. commonwealmagazine.org/print/38454
5 Mark J. Allman & Tobias L. Winright, *After the Smoke Clears: The Just War Tradition and Post War Justice* (Maryknoll, N.Y.: Orbis Books, 2010) p. 50.
6 See http://davidswanson.org and http://warisalie.org
7 Molly O'Toole, *Defense One,* "UN Ambassador Warns Against Intervention Fatigue," http://www.defenseone.com/ threats/2014/11/un-ambassador-warns-against-intervention-fatigue/99485/
8 Chris Hellman, *TomDispatch,* "$1.2 Trillion for National Security," March 1, 2011, http://www.tomdispatch.com/blog/175361
9 Chris Klimek, *Airspacemag.com,* "An Aerial Food Drop Over Syria Missed Its Target, and That's No Surprise," http://www. airspacemag.com/daily-planet/anatomy-high-altitude-air-drop-180958361/?no-ist
10 *Gallup,* "End of Year Survey 2013," http://www.wingia.com/en/ services/end_of_year_survey_2013/7
11 Talia Hagerty, *Pacific Standard,* "War Cost World $9.46 Trillion in 2012," republished by World Beyond War, http://worldbeyondwar. org/war-cost-world-9-46-trillion-2012/
12 Robert Pollin and Heidi Garrett-Peltier, "The U.S. Employment Effects of Military and Domestic Spending Priorities: 2011 Update," November 28, 2011, http://www.peri.umass.edu/236/hash/0b0ce 6af7ff999b11745825d80aca0b8/publication/489/

13 *National Priorities Project,* "Federal Discretionary Spending 2015," https://www.nationalpriorities.org/charts/partial/discretionary/

14 David Swanson, "But, Mr. Putin, You Just Don't Understand," http://davidswanson.org/node/5238 and Adam Johnson, FAIR, "NYT Reveals Think Tank It's Cited for Years to Be Corrupt Arms Booster," http://fair.org/home/nyt-reveals-think-tank-its-cited-for-years-to-be-corrupt-arms-booster and Lee Fang, *The Intercept,* "U.S. Defense Contractors Tell Investors Russian Threat Is Great for Business," https://theintercept.com/2016/08/19/nato-weapons-industry

15 David Sirota, *International Business Times,* "Clinton Foundation Donors Got Weapons Deals From Hillary Clinton's State Department," http://www.ibtimes.com/clinton-foundation-donors-got-weapons-deals-hillary-clintons-state-department-1934187

16 See the stats on a map at bit.ly/mappingmilitarism

17 Nabih Bulos , W.J. Hennigan, and Brian Bennett, *Los Angeles Times,* "In Syria, militias armed by the Pentagon fight those armed by the CIA," March 27, 2016, http://www.latimes.com/world/middleeast/la-fg-cia-pentagon-isis-20160327-story.html

18 David Swanson, "Pope Tells World's Top Arms Dealers to End Arms Trade," http://davidswanson.org/node/4921

19 C.J. Chivers, *New York Times,* "How Many Guns Did the U.S. Lose Track of in Iraq and Afghanistan? Hundreds of Thousands," http://www.nytimes.com/2016/08/23/magazine/how-many-guns-did-the-us-lose-track-of-in-iraq-and-afghanistan-hundreds-of-thousands.html

20 Find all of these quotes documented at http://warisacrime.org/lesssafe

21 Ewen MacAskill, *The Guardian,* "Fivefold increase in terrorism fatalities since 9/11, says report," https://www.theguardian.com/uk-news/2014/nov/18/fivefold-increase-terrorism-fatalities-global-index

22 *Gallup,* End of Year Survey 2014, http://www.wingia.com/en/services/end_of_year_survey_2014/8

23 Reports and photos from the Rome meeting: https://nonviolencejustpeace.net

24 John Horgan, *The End of War* (McSweeney's, 2012).

25 Farea Al-muslimi testimony at Drone Wars Senate Committee Hearing, https://www.youtube.com/watch?v=JtQ_mMKx3Ck

26 David Swanson, "Listen to Ex-CIA Officer Tell Me Killing Bin Laden Was Cleaner Than Capturing Him," http://davidswanson. org/content/listen-ex-cia-officer-tell-me-killing-bin-laden-was-cleaner-capturing-him

27 *The Intercept,* "The Drone Papers," https://theintercept.com/ drone-papers/ and for an independent study that puts the figure at 96% of drone victims being unknown see http://www.reprieve.org. uk/press/2014_11_25_us_drone_strikes_kill_28_each_target

28 Mark J. Allman & Tobias L. Winright, *After the Smoke Clears: The Just War Tradition and Post War Justice* (Maryknoll, N.Y.: Orbis Books, 2010) p. 9.

29 "Madeleine Albright says 500,000 dead Iraqi Children was 'worth it,' wins Medal of Freedom," https://www.youtube.com/ watch?v=omnskeu-puE

30 *Politico,* Coverage of the fifth GOP presidential debate, http:// www.politico.com/blogs/live-from-the-venetian/2015/12/hugh-hewitt-ben-carson-innocent-children-war-216820#ixzz44Vp2NEpl

31 Mark J. Allman and Tobias Winright, "Protect Thy Neighbor," Commonweal Magazine, June 2, 2016, https://www. commonwealmagazine.org/print/38454

32 David Carroll Cochran, *Catholic Realism and the Abolition of War* (Orbis Books, 2014).

33 David Swanson, "Amnesty International Once Again Refuses to Oppose War," http://davidswanson.org/node/4941

34 See videos at http://hillaryisaneocon.com. Also see: Sarah Westwood, *Washington Examiner,* "Six Things We Learned from the Blumenthal Emails," June 24, 2015, http://washex.am/1NCxz1l

35 Pentagon Papers, http://www.archives.gov/research/pentagon-papers

36 Jim Lobe, *Inter Press Service,* "So, Did Saddam Hussein Try to Kill Bush's Dad?" October 19, 2004. Accessed October 7, 2010, http:// russbaker.com/archives/Guerrilla percent20News percent20Network percent20- percent20Bush.htm

37 Ewen MacAskill, *The Guardian,* "George Bush: 'God told me to end the tyranny in Iraq,'" October 7, 2005. Accessed October 7, 2010, http://www.guardian.co.uk/world/2005/oct/07/iraq.usa.

38 Dennis Perrin, *Savage Mules: The Democrats and Endless War,* (Brooklyn: Verso, 2008).

39 Irina Slav, *OilPrice.com,* "Chilcot Report: UK Oil Interests Were Lead Motive For Iraq War," http://finance.yahoo.com/news/

chilcot-report-uk-oil-interests-151700491.html and David Whyte and Greg Muttitt, *Open Democracy*, "Chilcot's blind spot: Iraq War report buries oil evidence, fails to address motive," https://www.opendemocracy.net/david-whyte/chilcot-s-oil-blind-spot-in-iraq-war-report

40 See these sources:

http://www.ibtimes.com/medicating-our-troops-oblivion-prescription-drugs-said-be-endangering-us-soldiers-1572217

http://legacy.sandiegouniontribune.com/news/military/20060319-9999-1n19mental.html

http://www.naturalnews.com/033241_soldiers_antipsychotic_drugs.html

http://www.veterans.senate.gov/imo/media/doc/For the Record - CCHR 4.30.14.pdf

http://www.nbcnews.com/id/30748260/ns/health-health_care/t/us-military-heavily-armed-medicated/#.VzaePteBZIc

41 Mark J. Allman & Tobias L. Winright, *After the Smoke Clears: The Just War Tradition and Post War Justice* (Maryknoll, N.Y.: Orbis Books, 2010) p. 16.

42 David Swanson, "If a Genocide Falls in the Forest," http://davidswanson.org/node/4476

43 John Caruso, "Support the Troops?" http://tinyrevolution.com/mt/archives/003243.html

44 David Swanson, "Sociocide: Iraq Is No More," http://davidswanson.org/content/sociocide-iraq-no-more

45 Bill Van Auken, "U.S. Soldier in WikiLeaks Video: I Relive This Every Day," http://www.wsws.org/en/articles/2010/04/emcc-a28.html

46 James Bovard, "Iraqi Sanctions and American Intentions," http://fff.org/explore-freedom/article/iraqi-sanctions-american-intentions-blameless-carnage-part-1

47 JPat Brown, "Who Would Jesus Nuke?" https://www.muckrock.com/news/archives/2016/aug/17/who-would-jesus-nuke-wwjn-air-force-chaplains-bann

48 Norman Solomon, *War Made Easy: How Presidents and Pundits Keep Spinning Us to Death* (Hoboken: John Wiley & Sons, 2005) 22-24.

49 "Madeleine Albright says 500,000 dead Iraqi Children was 'worth it,' wins Medal of Freedom," https://www.youtube.com/watch?v=omnskeu-puE

50 David Swanson, "Study Finds People Assume War Is Only Last Resort," http://davidswanson.org/node/4637

51 Nicolas Davies, *Alternet*, "Armed Rebels and Middle-Eastern Power Plays: How the U.S. Is Helping to Kill Peace in Syria," http://www.alternet.org/world/armed-rebels-and-middle-eastern-power-plays-how-us-helping-kill-peace-syria

52 Julian Borger and Bastien Inzaurralde, "West 'ignored Russian offer in 2012 to have Syria's Assad step aside,'" https://www.theguardian.com/world/2015/sep/15/west-ignored-russian-offer-in-2012-to-have-syrias-assad-step-aside

53 Farea Al-muslimi testimony at Drone Wars Senate Committee Hearing, https://www.youtube.com/watch?v=JtQ_mMKx3Ck

54 *The Mirror*, "Navy Seal Rob O'Neill who killed Osama bin Laden claims US had no intention of capturing terrorist," http://www.mirror.co.uk/news/world-news/navy-seal-rob-oneill-who-4612012 See also: *ABC News*, "Osama Bin Laden Unarmed When Killed, White House Says," http://abcnews.go.com/Blotter/osama-bin-laden-unarmed-killed-white-house/story?id=13520152

55 *The Washington Post*, "Gaddafi accepts road map for peace proposed by African leaders," https://www.washingtonpost.com/world/african-leaders-arrive-in-libya-in-attempt-to-broker-cease-fire-gaddafi-hopes-for-sympathy/2011/04/10/AF0VH6ED_story.html

56 See http://warisacrime.org/whitehousememo

57 Julian Borger in Washington, Brian Whitaker and Vikram Dodd, *The Guardian*, "Saddam's desperate offers to stave off war," https://www.theguardian.com/world/2003/nov/07/iraq.brianwhitaker

58 Julian Borger in Washington, Brian Whitaker and Vikram Dodd, *The Guardian*, "Saddam's desperate offers to stave off war," https://www.theguardian.com/world/2003/nov/07/iraq.brianwhitaker

59 Julian Borger in Washington, Brian Whitaker and Vikram Dodd, *The Guardian*, "Saddam's desperate offers to stave off war," https://www.theguardian.com/world/2003/nov/07/iraq.brianwhitaker

60 Memo of meeting: https://en.wikisource.org/wiki/Bush-Aznar_memo and news report: Jason Webb, *Reuters*, "Bush thought Saddam was prepared to flee: report," http://www.reuters.com/article/us-iraq-bush-spain-idUSL2683831120070926

61 Rory McCarthy, *The Guardian*, "New offer on Bin Laden," https://www.theguardian.com/world/2001/oct/17/afghanistan.terrorism11

62 Clyde Haberman, *New York Times,* "Pope Denounces the Gulf War as 'Darkness'," http://www.nytimes.com/1991/04/01/world/pope-denounces-the-gulf-war-as-darkness.html

63 David Swanson, *War Is A Lie,* http://warisalie.org

64 White House Memo: http://warisacrime.org/whitehousememo

65 Mark J. Allman & Tobias L. Winright, *After the Smoke Clears: The Just War Tradition and Post War Justice* (Maryknoll, N.Y.: Orbis Books, 2010) p. 43.

66 Department of Justice White Paper, http://msnbcmedia.msn.com/i/msnbc/sections/news/020413_DOJ_White_Paper.pdf

67 2002 National Security Strategy, http://www.globalsecurity.org/military/library/policy/national/nss-020920.pdf

68 Erica Chenoweth and Maria J. Stephan, *Why Civil Resistance Works: The Strategic Logic of Nonviolent Conflict* (Columbia University Press, 2012).

69 Stephen Zunes, "Alternatives to War from the Bottom Up," http://www.filmsforaction.org/articles/alternatives-to-war-from-the-bottom-up/

70 Mark J. Allman & Tobias L. Winright, *After the Smoke Clears: The Just War Tradition and Post War Justice* (Maryknoll, N.Y.: Orbis Books, 2010) p. 9.

71 Mikhail Gorbachev, The New Russia, (Polity, 2016).

72 Mark J. Allman & Tobias L. Winright, *After the Smoke Clears: The Just War Tradition and Post War Justice* (Maryknoll, N.Y.: Orbis Books, 2010) p. 8.

73 Mark J. Allman & Tobias L. Winright, *After the Smoke Clears: The Just War Tradition and Post War Justice* (Maryknoll, N.Y.: Orbis Books, 2010) pp. 40-41.

74 David Swanson, *When the World Outlawed War,* (Charlottesville: David Swanson, 2011).

75 Barack Obama, "Address on Drones and Terrorism at the National Defense University," 23 May 2013, Fort McNair, Washington, D.C., http://www.americanrhetoric.com/speeches/barackobama/barackobamanationaldefenseuniversity.htm

76 *The Intercept,* "The Drone Papers," https://theintercept.com/drone-papers/ and for an independent study that puts the figure at 96% of drone victims being unknown see http://www.reprieve.org.uk/press/2014_11_25_us_drone_strikes_kill_28_each_target

77 Farea Al-muslimi testimony at Drone Wars Senate Committee Hearing, https://www.youtube.com/watch?v=JtQ_mMKx3Ck

78 *The Intercept,* "The Drone Papers," https://theintercept.com/drone-papers/ and for an independent study that puts the figure at 96% of drone victims being unknown see http://www.reprieve.org.uk/press/2014_11_25_us_drone_strikes_kill_28_each_target

79 Dwight Eisenhower, Farewell Address, 1961, http://www.pbs.org/wgbh/americanexperience/features/primary-resources/eisenhower-farewell/

80 David Swanson, "Killer Drone Lovers Have Their Movie," http://davidswanson.org/eye

81 *Wikipedia,* Ticking Time Bomb Scenario, https://en.wikipedia.org/wiki/Ticking_time_bomb_scenario

82 Jo Becker and Scott Shane, *New York Times,* "Secret 'Kill List' Proves a Test of Obama's Principles and Will," May 29, 2012, http://www.nytimes.com/2012/05/29/world/obamas-leadership-in-war-on-al-qaeda.html?_r=0

83 *Christian Science Monitor,* Sudanese Factory Destroyed by U.S. Now a Shrine, http://www.csmonitor.com/World/Africa/2012/0807/Sudanese-factory-destroyed-by-US-now-a-shrine

84 David Swanson, "How the Pentagon Removes Entire Peoples," http://davidswanson.org/node/4058

85 Mark J. Allman & Tobias L. Winright, *After the Smoke Clears: The Just War Tradition and Post War Justice* (Maryknoll, N.Y.: Orbis Books, 2010) p. 9, footnote 20.

86 Mark J. Allman & Tobias L. Winright, *After the Smoke Clears: The Just War Tradition and Post War Justice* (Maryknoll, N.Y.: Orbis Books, 2010) p. 141.

87 Michael Walzer, *New York Times,* What a Little War in Iraq Could Do, March 7, 2003, http://www.nytimes.com/2003/03/07/opinion/what-a-little-war-in-iraq-could-do.html

88 David Swanson, "The Democratic Push to Bomb Iraq Again," http://davidswanson.org/node/4430

89 John Hanrahan, "Duping Progressives into Wars," https://consortiumnews.com/2016/04/14/duping-progressives-into-wars and Molly Ball, "Why a Democrat Who Opposed the Iraq War Backs Intervening in Syria," http://www.theatlantic.com/politics/archive/2013/08/why-a-democrat-who-opposed-the-iraq-war-backs-intervening-in-syria/279221

90 Tom Perriello, "Humanitarian Intervention: Recognizing When, and Why, It Can Succeed," http://www.democracyjournal.org/23/

humanitarian-intervention-recognizing-when-and-why-it-can-succeed.php?page=all

91 Mark J. Allman & Tobias L. Winright, *After the Smoke Clears: The Just War Tradition and Post War Justice* (Maryknoll, N.Y.: Orbis Books, 2010) p. 88.

92 *Associated Press,* "Wolfowitz comments revive doubts over Iraq's WMD," http://usatoday30.usatoday.com/news/world/iraq/2003-05-30-wolfowitz-iraq_x.htm

93 Thirty-Five Articles of Impeachment Against George W. Bush, http://warisacrime.org/busharticles

94 Phyllis Bennis, *Institute for Policy Studies,* "February 15, 2003. The Day the World Said No to War," http://www.ips-dc.org/february_15_2003_the_day_the_world_said_no_to_war

95 Thirty-Five Articles of Impeachment Against George W. Bush, http://warisacrime.org/busharticles

96 *The Guardian*, "Chilcot report: key points from the Iraq inquiry," https://www.theguardian.com/uk-news/2016/jul/06/iraq-inquiry-key-points-from-the-chilcot-report

97 Mark J. Allman & Tobias L. Winright, *After the Smoke Clears: The Just War Tradition and Post War Justice* (Maryknoll, N.Y.: Orbis Books, 2010) p. 8.

98 Tom Boggioni, *Raw Story,* "Meet the Christian Leader Who Wants You to Vote for Trump," http://www.rawstory.com/2016/08/meet-the-christian-leader-who-wants-you-to-vote-for-trump-because-hell-bring-the-second-coming

99 Mark J. Allman and Tobias Winright, *Commonweal Magazine,* "Protect Thy Neighbor," June 2, 2016, https://www.commonwealmagazine.org/print/38454

100 *Pax Christi,* "Nonviolence Conference: Message from Pope Francis at the opening of the conference on nonviolence and just peace," https://paxchristiusa.org/2016/04/12/nonviolence-conference-message-from-pope-francis-at-the-opening-of-the-conference-on-nonviolence-and-just-peace/

101 Joshua J. McElwee, *National Catholic Reporter,* "Vatican to host first-ever conference to reevaluate just war theory, justifications for violence," https://www.ncronline.org/news/global/vatican-host-first-ever-conference-reevaluate-just-war-theory-justifications-violence

102 Reports and photos from the Rome meeting: https://nonviolencejustpeace.net

103 The Nonviolence and Just Peace Conference Statement, https://nonviolencejustpeace.net/final-statement-an-appeal-to-the-catholic-church-to-re-commit-to-the-centrality-of-gospel-nonviolence

104 http://press.vatican.va/content/salastampa/it/bollettino/pubblico/2016/08/26/0599/01345.html

105 http://www.scborromeo.org/ccc/p3s2c2a5.htm

106 http://www.vatican.va/archive/hist_councils/ii_vatican_council/documents/vat-ii_cons_19651207_gaudium-et-spes_en.html

107 Mark J. Allman & Tobias L. Winright, *After the Smoke Clears: The Just War Tradition and Post War Justice* (Maryknoll, N.Y.: Orbis Books, 2010) p. 53.

108 Talk Nation Radio: Mel Duncan on why unarmed civilian protection is better than war, http://davidswanson.org/node/5203

109 Studs Terkel, *The Good War: An Oral History of World War II* (The New Press: 1997).

110 Chris Hellman, *TomDispatch*, "$1.2 Trillion for National Security," March 1, 2011, http://www.tomdispatch.com/blog/175361

111 David Swanson, *War Is A Lie,* Second Edition (Charlottesville: Just World Books, 2016).

112 Mark J. Allman & Tobias L. Winright, *After the Smoke Clears: The Just War Tradition and Post War Justice* (Maryknoll, N.Y.: Orbis Books, 2010) p. 46.

113 Mark J. Allman & Tobias L. Winright, *After the Smoke Clears: The Just War Tradition and Post War Justice* (Maryknoll, N.Y.: Orbis Books, 2010) p. 14.

114 Mark J. Allman & Tobias L. Winright, *After the Smoke Clears: The Just War Tradition and Post War Justice* (Maryknoll, N.Y.: Orbis Books, 2010) p. 97.

115 *War No More: Three Centuries of American Antiwar and Peace Writing*, edited by Lawrence Rosendwald.

116 David Swanson, *War Is A Lie,* Second Edition (Charlottesville: Just World Books, 2016).

117 Book and Film: *A Force More Powerful,* http://aforcemorepowerful.org

118 Dave Grossman, *On Killing: The Psychological Cost of Learning to Kill in War and Society* (Back Bay Books: 1996).

119 Donald G. McNeil Jr., *The New York Times*, "U.S. Apologizes for

Syphilis Tests in Guatemala," October 1, 2010, http://www.nytimes.com/2010/10/02/health/research/02infect.html

120 Annie Jacobsen, *Operation Paperclip: The Secret Intelligence Program that Brought Nazi Scientists to America* (Little, Brown and Company, 2014).

121 Oliver Stone and Peter Kuznick, *The Untold History of the United States* (Gallery Books, 2013).

122 Steven A. Bank, Kirk J. Stark, and Joseph J. Thorndike, *War and Taxes* (Urban Institute Press, 2008).

123 *RootsAction.org*, "Move Away from Nonstop War. Close the Ramstein Air Base," http://act.rootsaction.org/p/dia/action3/common/public/?action_KEY=12254

124 David Swanson, "The United States Just Bombed Germany," http://davidswanson.org/node/5134

125 Howard Zinn, *A People's History of the United States* (Harper Perennial Modern Classics; Reissue edition, November 17, 2015).

126 Shaila Dewandec, *New York Times*, "When the Germans, and Rockets, Came to Town," December 31, 2007, http://www.nytimes.com/2007/12/31/us/31huntsville.html

127 Annie Jacobsen, *Operation Paperclip: The Secret Intelligence Program that Brought Nazi Scientists to America* (Little, Brown and Company, 2014).

128 See *Costs of Major U.S. Wars*, by the Congressional Research Service, June 29, 2010.

129 Ta-Nehisi Coates, *The Atlantic*, "No, Lincoln Could Not Have 'Bought the Slaves'," June 20, 2013, http://www.theatlantic.com/national/archive/2013/06/no-lincoln-could-not-have-bought-the-slaves/277073

130 Andy Wilcoxson, *Counter Punch*, The Exoneration of Milosevic: the ICTY's Surprise Ruling, http://www.counterpunch.org/2016/08/01/the-exoneration-of-milosevic-the-ictys-surprise-ruling

131 Diana Johnstone, *Fools' Crusade: Yugoslavia, NATO and Western Delusions* (Monthly Review Press, 2002).

132 *Fairness and Accuracy in Reporting*, "What Reporters Knew About Kosovo Talks But Didn't Tell," http://fair.org/press-release/what-reporters-knew-about-kosovo-talks8212but-didnt-tell

133 On the NATO Bombing of Yugoslavia, Noam Chomsky interviewed by Danilo Mandic, RTS Online, April 25, 2006, https://chomsky.info/20060425

134 Testimony of Harold Hongju Koh, Legal Advisor U.S.
Department of State, Testimony Before the Senate Foreign
Relations Committee, Washington, D.C., June 28, 2011, http://www.
state.gov/s/l/releases/remarks/167250.htm and Paul Starobin,
New York Times, "A Moral Flip-Flop? Defining a War," August 6, 2011,
http://www.nytimes.com/2011/08/07/opinion/sunday/harold-
kohs-flip-flop-on-the-libya-question.html
135 Chris Hedges, *TruthDig,* "Libya: Here We Go Again," September
5, 2011, http://bit.ly/1RYgnsv
136 *YnetNews,* "Libya says any attack would threaten
Mediterranean," 17 March 2011, http://www.ynetnews.com/
articles/0,7340,L-4044011,00.html
137 Alan J. Kuperman, *The Boston Globe,* "False pretense for war in
Libya?," April 14, 2011, http://archive.boston.com/bostonglobe/
editorial_opinion/oped/articles/2011/04/14/false_pretense_for_
war_in_libya/
138 See videos at http://hillaryisaneocon.com. Also see: Sarah
Westwood, *Washington Examiner,* "Six Things We Learned from the
Blumenthal Emails," June 24, 2015, http://washex.am/1NCxz1l
139 Robert Parry, *Consortium News,* "Hillary Clinton's Failed Libya
'Doctrine'," July 1, 2015, http://bit.ly/1Iey19o
140 Talk Nation Radio: The Congo and the U.S.-Backed Deadliest
Conflict Since WWII, http://davidswanson.org/node/4299
141 Mark J. Allman & Tobias L. Winright, *After the Smoke Clears:
The Just War Tradition and Post War Justice* (Maryknoll, N.Y.: Orbis
Books, 2010) p. 156.
142 World Beyond War, *A Global Security System: An Alternative to
War,* http://worldbeyondwar.org/alternative
143 Chris Klimek, *Airspacemag.com,* "An Aerial Food Drop Over
Syria Missed Its Target, and That's No Surprise," http://www.
airspacemag.com/daily-planet/anatomy-high-altitude-air-drop-
180958361/?no-ist

CPSIA information can be obtained
at www.ICGtesting.com
Printed in the USA
LVOW01s1120021016
507071LV00013B/377/P